STEPPING *into* FAVOR

ACCESS GOD'S TIMELESS BLESSINGS

JOLYNNE WHITTAKER

© 2017 Clarion Call, LLC

Book Author: Jolynne Whittaker
Book Title: Stepping Into Favor
All rights reserved. No part of this publication may be reproduced, stored in a retrieval system or transmitted in any form or by any means, electronic, mechanical, photocopying, recording or otherwise without the prior permision of the publisher or in accordance with the provisions of the Copyright, Designs and Patents Act 1988 or under the terms of any licence permitting limited copying issued by the Copyright Licensing Angency.

Published by: Clarion Call, LLC for JoLynne Whittaker Ministries

ISBN-10: 0-9991197-0-2

ISBN-13: 978-0-9991197-0-9

STEPPING *into* FAVOR

ACCESS GOD'S TIMELESS BLESSINGS

Dedication

First and foremost, this book is dedicated as a sacrifice to my Lord and Savior, Jesus Christ. Without the love and hope of Christ, I don't know where I'd be. I can never repay the Lord Jesus for all he's done for me, but I can use what he gave me to help others, and that is my intention regarding *Stepping Into Favor*.

Next, I'd like to dedicate this book to *you*. To the wonderful individual who is about to unlock the promises of God, perhaps by seeing favor in a way you've never seen it before.

Yes, this book is dedicated to *you*, the person who is about to access the timeless blessings of God and the protocols required to access them. You're about to empower yourself to step into favor, and I couldn't be more excited for you!

Whatever your situation in life, stepping into God's favor can make it better. However well you're doing right now, the favor of God can add to your life in simply unimaginable ways! However badly you're struggling or suffering right now, God's favor is more than able to sweep into your life like a cleansing wind and clear away anything that is blocking you from living according to His highest will for you.

Stepping into the favor of the Lord changed my life. I know it can and will change yours, too. I encourage you to look up every Scripture I quote; this will help you to comprehend the reality and gravity of the Lord's desire for you to step into favor! And when you do, I encourage you to do three vital things. First, give God glory! Second, tell someone what God did for you — let your testimony increase their faith. Third, bless someone else the way God blessed you. Let the Lord use you to be someone's miracle.

Finally, this book is dedicated to my mother. Mom, I know you tried with all you knew, to break out of poverty and financial instability, but could not. Someday you'll know that I did it for us, Mom. I broke the cycles, I broke the curse! I'll tell you all about it, when I see you in heaven. Until then, I'm going to help as many people as I can to break their cycles, too.

- JoLynne Whittaker

TABLE OF CONTENTS

INTRODUCTION..1

1 - NEPOTISM - FAVOR THE WRONG WAY 5

2 - GODLY FAVOR...9

3 - PROSPERITY - OF GOD OR NOT?...17

4 - POVERTY IS SATANIC..35

5 - FAVOR IS GOD'S PROMISE..49

6 - OBEDIENCE IS A SETUP!..57

7 - FAVOR WHEREVER YOU GO 65

8 - FAVOR AND BLESSING FOR YOUR CHILDREN.............69

9 - HE BLESSES YOUR EFFORTS!...77

10 - HIS SAFETY SHALL SURROUND YOU LIKE A SHIELD..............87

11 - HIS FAVOR SHALL PROTECT YOU FROM YOUR ENEMIES.......91

12 - HE WILL BLESS YOUR HOLDINGS, AND PURSUITS...................99

13 - THERE IS POWER IN CONCECRATION AND OBEDIENCE...111

14 - YOU'RE ABOUT TO STEP INTO FEAR-INSPIRING FAVOR!....121

15 - SUPERNATURAL INCREASE OF HOLDINGS AND CHILDREN..127

16 - ABUNDANTLY PROSPEROUS AND DEBT FREE 133

17 - STRONG, FREE, EMPOWERED --- THAT'S YOU! 145

18 - GOD EXPECTS YOUR LOYALTY IN RETURN...............151

19 - STEP INTO FAVOR AND STAY THERE!............................157

20 - A SPECIAL MESSAGE FROM JOLYNNE WHITTAKER..............163

Introduction

After reading and studying my Bible, I believe God's favor is the birthright of every faithful born again believer in Jesus Christ. I also believe your adversary, the devil, desires to keep you from that favor.

The favor of God is not some far-off, mysterious blessing that requires great effort to obtain. Rather, God's favor is the simple yet glorious 'benefits package' the Lord offers each His children, most generously.

In this book, I am exposing Satan's deliberate plan to keep you ignorant of the favor you are entitled to, and the diabolical strategy frequently used to keep humans incapable of accessing it.

I'm also answering these questions: What is the favor of God? Where can we find examples of God's favor, in the Bible? How does one step into favor? When God's favor shows up in your life, what does it look like? Will the favor of God improve your life?

These are great questions, let's dive in!

God wants you to step into His favor. He wants you to live in freedom and security. The Lord wants you to be blessed, and He wants to empower you to be a blessing to others. Stepping into God's favor will allow you to do that. Are you ready to learn how? Let's begin!

— JoLynne Whittaker

Chapter One
Nepotism - Favor The Wrong Way

Favor is a word that has both a positive and a negative connotation, is it not? We've heard folks accuse others of receiving a victory or success unfairly, because someone *favored* them. We've seen instances where the outcome, ruling, or promotion was unfair, because someone was the recipient of nepotism, which is unjust favor. So too have we seen instances where someone has gone from the back to the front very quickly, or from the bottom to the top very quickly — because of (say it with me) *favor.*

It's true, favor isn't always fair. Favor is the dispensation of privilege or opportunity upon someone by someone else, whether they deserved it or not.

When favor is dispensed in the secular realm, such as via the justice or scholastic systems or within a popular industry, there is the very real possibility that someone received their 'break' or opportunity, because of nepotism. In those instances, the dispensation of favor is completely unjust. After all, who's to say there wasn't a more qualified or deserving candidate?

Nepotism
*/ nepe, tizem/ — noun
the practice among those with power or influence of favoring relatives or friends, especially by giving them jobs. favoritism, preferential treatment bias, partiality, partisanship*

Yet, that's what nepotism does: it doles out promotion, payouts, promises and prosperity to whomever it chooses, regardless of whether it's justified or correct to do so.

Have you ever seen this? It can be maddening! Someone in power will simply promote whomever they choose, they'll favor whomever they will, and there's nothing anyone (who doesn't have the authority and power to challenge it) can do about it.

Please don't miss that relevant nugget: in order to dispense favor, even in the form of nepotism, *one must be in a position of authority and power.*

When humans dispense favor, it's a crapshoot, for lack of a better term. It may be just, it may be unjust; the human in charge gets to decide. Those involved are at the mercy of the one in power.

The favor of God, however, is an entirely different entity. Let's learn about it.

Chapter Two
Godly Favor

The favor of God manifests itself in various ways, all of them scriptural and entirely appropriate. The sovereign God who created this earth and all human beings on it, is legally able to dispense favor at His own disposal, because as Creator, God can favor whomever He chooses, whenever He chooses.

The very definition of the word 'favor' itself, indicates what God's favor can mean in your life:

Favor
fa-vor (fa'ver) — noun
A gracious, friendly, or obliging act that is freely granted Friendly or favorable regard; approval or support. A state of being held in good regard, as the recipient of a benefit or goodwill

Wow! Yes please, Lord! I'll take it! How about you? If you could have God invade your life regularly, simply to give you favor, how would that be? If you could have the Lord show up for you routinely to help you, extend friendly advantages to you, create favorable outcomes for you, would you like that?

In *Psalm 5:12* the Bible refers to the favor of God functioning like a shield, which means it can protect us.

Later, in *Psalm 84:11*, the psalmist David reveals what else the favor 'shield' of God can provide: it gives grace and glory, withholding no good thing from those who walk uprightly.

In the Book of Esther, we learn how the favor of God can influence the way others respond to us, even if we're among enemies in hostile territory! - *Esther 2:15-18*

This is later enforced in *Luke 2:52* where we read about the upbringing of Jesus Christ himself. That verse reports how Jesus grew in wisdom and stature, and *in favor with God and man*.

God's favor is incredibly relevant. Favor from the Lord can make all the difference. Indeed, God's favor can be life-changing, quite literally.

Just one touch of God's favor can alter the health and functionality of your family.

Just one touch of God's favor can improve

your financial situation.

Just one touch of God's favor can change your career status.

Just one touch of God's favor can cause you to live healthy and long.

On and on... for there is no end to what God's favor can do!

I don't know about you, but I need this. I don't want to live my life relying on my own good ideas or my own savvy. I don't want to rely on my own ability to pry open doors and create sustainable business expressions. No thank you, I do not wish to rely solely on my ability to brainstorm real-life solutions that are effective for my household.

I want the favor of God on my life!

I want to do whatever it takes to access God's timeless blessings!

I want to do whatever it takes to step into God's favor!

My friends, I have lived without God's favor, and I have lived with it. I prefer to live with it! Once you've experienced the favor of the Lord, I'm confident you will share that perspective!

God-sized favor is big. God-sized favor can be a supernatural game-changer, the stuff of legacies and generational blessing.

What if I told you there is a relatively small but loaded portion of Scripture wherein God details exactly what God-sized favor looks like, *as a package?* Some employers offer a benefits package to employees; some parents offer an inheritance package to their children — *what if I told you God has designed the ultimate benefit and inheritance package, for YOU?*
And what if I told you that package is extended as a gift to every loyal believer and follower of Jesus Christ?
My friends, it's true. In the coming chapters, we're going to examine that portion of Scripture, verse by verse.

But first, we need to challenge the misconception that prosperity is wrong or somehow unholy. We also need to define and clarify Biblical prosperity.

By the time you finish the last page of this book, I want to have equipped and motivated you to step into the favor of God — so your life can shift in a significant way.

What's my angle?

No angle, my friend. Quite simply, having been raised very poor, I am passionate about helping God's people obtain their rightful portion of God's favor — and that includes financial blessing.

Favor is your inheritance, Christian.

I am simply the vessel God is using in this season, to help you access that inheritance.

I find it offensive that many Christians today walk in ongoing struggle or generational lack, even poverty. I find that offensive because that is not who our God is. Poverty and ongoing financial lack is not God's wish for you. *- Jeremiah 29:11, Philippians 4:19*

As I have ministered to people all over the world, I have noticed consistently that many people have mental blocks in place. Those mental blocks can stall or hinder financial growth.

The Bible teaches: *As a man thinketh, so is he… - Proverbs 23:7*

Therefore, the way you think about financial stability, prosperity, even the acquisition of personal wealth, directly affects your ability to receive or create it.

Bear with me, I need to repeat that: *The way you think about financial stability, prosperity, and the acquisition of personal wealth, directly affects your ability to receive or create it.*

I know this is one hundred percent true because I have observed this mindset at work in people all over the world, and I have lived it, myself.

The Bible shows us God's habit of appointing a leader, speaker, prophet or worker whenever He needs to get a job done. He did so with Moses, Noah, Jonah, the apostles, and so many others.

For the entirety of this book, I'm going to be that person for you. The time we spend together as you read *Stepping Into Favor,* will be like a personal journey. As we journey together through the pages of this book, I'll be helping you to clarify your understanding of God's favor, and I'll be helping you position yourself to step into that favor.

Unlike human favor, the Lord's favor has no strings attached. Being the recipient of God's favor may make the devil mad, and it may stir up contention or murmurings from folks who are, simply put, jealous. But God will never demand something from you as *payment* for His favor.

Rather, God lays out the following simple requirement to all who would receive His wonderful favor: *If ye be willing and obedient, ye shall eat the good of the land… - Isaiah 1:19*

Fair enough, don't you think? All God asks in advance, is that we love and obey Him.

Are you ready to learn more?
If so, turn the page.
Let's begin by tackling the prosperity issue.

Chapter Three
Prosperity - Of God Or Not?

Throughout the Bible, we see God's clear and consistent style of blessing: The Lord blesses His faithful and obedient children with land, homes, resources, health, wealth, and the acumen required to cultivate or acquire such things.

Both stability and abundance are important to God. He desires for you to be secure, yet He also desires for you to be in a position to aid and bless others. Jehovah Jireh is the God of provision, but He is also the God of abundant overflow. - *Genesis 22:14, Malachi 3:10*

Allow me to say with Holy Ghost infused boldness and confidence: wealth, generational promises of wellbeing and prosperity, financial stability and overflow — *all these things are of God.*

Again, favor from a secular source may come with strings attached. You may find yourself owing someone a favor in return, if they extend a favor to you.

Or, you may find yourself indebted to that individual, now at their mercy or under their control.

Godly favor is not contaminated by such debased and sinful demands.

Your Bible says God wants you to prosper, He wants you to succeed. He has only well-wishes for you. The Lord does not desire His loyal and faithful children to suffer, struggle, or go without. *- Jeremiah 29:11*

Poverty breeds a pervasive atmosphere of desperation and fear. I should know, I grew up in poverty, surrounded by other impoverished people. Poverty isn't pretty, nor does it breed pretty behaviors.

The desperation that comes with an ongoing impoverished lifestyle causes people to act irrationally. That same desperation, fueled by a lack of finances, often drives people to do things that are erratic, dangerous, uncharacteristic of their normal behavior — just to provide for their needs.

This is the exact opposite of God's plan for the environ of your mind and atmosphere of your home.

Poverty causes one to live in fear, because it robs you of your stability, confidence, freedom and empowerment.

I recall how instability and fear pervaded the neighborhood in which I grew up. This is in contrast with God's wish for us. *2 Timothy 1:7 says: For God has not given us the spirit of fear; but of power, and of love, and of a sound mind.*

Poverty or financial disadvantage causes the absence of basic human provision: food, someplace to call 'home', a spirit that is calm and at peace. The absence of these things is where the fear comes from. There is no peace, because there's simply too much instability.

John 14:27 says: Peace I leave with you, My peace I give you; not as the world gives do I give to you. Let not your heart be troubled, neither let it be afraid.

Philippians 4:6-7 says: Be anxious for nothing, but in everything by prayer and supplication, with thanksgiving, let your requests be made known to God; and the peace of God, which surpasses all understanding, will guard your hearts and minds through Christ Jesus.

*Poverty is the devil's wish for you.
Prosperity is God's wish for you.
Which do you prefer?*

My friend, financial struggle, fear, poverty and lack are products of Satan's world, not God's.

The Word of God makes this clear. God's

Word also makes it clear that under Satan's system, our peace and provision will be attacked.
-*John 10:10*

Therefore, the Lord has created provision: His favor.
Glory to God!

We learn from the stunning and utterly breathtaking structure of the garden of Eden, exactly what God intended for us: abundance, provision, enjoyment, a life lacking nothing.

The garden of Eden was beautiful! The garden was loaded with good things to eat! Adam and Eve wanted for nothing! They had animals for companionship and entertainment. Any food they craved to satisfy a savory or sweet tooth, was literally at their fingertips.
No stress. No worry. No fear. No lack. No wondering where they were going to live, what uncertainties tomorrow would bring, what they were going to eat, or how they were going to pay for it.

That, my friends, is God's wish, His way.
Under the Lord's rule and leadership, we have what we need, and more.
Please begin to associate abundance with God.

Please begin to associate overflow with God.
Please begin to associate a life of plenty and so much more than enough, with God.
Because life and life more abundantly is exactly what Jesus came to give us, as that is God's way! Abundance is the Lord's style! - *John 10:10, Philippians 4:19*

Webster's dictionary defines prosperity thus:

Prosperity
pros-per-i-ty (pros'par'itty) — noun
The state of being prosperous; advance or gain in anything good or desirable; successful progress in any business or enterprise; attainment of the object desired; good fortune; success...

But how does the Bible define prosperity? Let's look at that.

The word *prosper* appears 49 times in the King James version of the Bible. The word *prospered* papers 13 times. The word *prospereth* appears 4 times. The word *prosperity* appears 17 times.

Now catch this: all forms of the Greek

and Hebrew words for all such references and variations combined, appear *125 times in the Old and New Testaments.*

What do we learn from this? *God is interested in prosperity.*

But what is *His* definition of it? To understand fully, we must go to the Greek and Hebrew languages. Join me in a brief word study, as doing so will greatly expand and solidify your base of knowledge and accurate understanding as it regards to Biblical prosperity.

Greek
(1) Euporia - *wealth, gain*
Note: It is from this word that the English language gets its' word euphoria, which means a state of bliss.
(2) Timios - *expensiveness, magnificence, costliness*
(3) Soteria - *deliverance, salvation, welfare, preservation*
(4) Perisseuo - *to be over and above, to abound, to have more than enough, increasing, lavished*
(5) Autarkies - *self-sufficient, sufficient*
(6) Eirene - *one, peace, quietness, rest*

Hebrew
(1) Korsharah - *prosperity*
(2) Shalu - *ease, prosperity*
(3) Shelevah - *ease, prosperity*
(4) Shelam - *welfare, prosperity*

(5) Shalvah - *quietness, ease*
(6) Shalom - *completeness, soundness, welfare, peace*
(7) Yeshuvah - *salvation*
(8) Tsedeq - *rightness, righteousness*
(9) Towb - *pleasant, agreeable, good*
(10) Yimnah - *good fortune*

Reader, from the number of words used in the original Greek and Hebrew to describe prosperity, all of which occur in the Bible, we can see that prosperity is definitely on God's mind.

We see that Biblical prosperity (that is, prosperity the way God intends for our lives) produces personal contentment and well-being. Prosperity from the Lord produces peace and an inner calm.

Prosperity from the Lord provides above and beyond all we need and ask, because God desires to see us in possession of overflow — so we can give and live freely, with ease. - *Ephesians 3:20*

Did you notice that those word studies that prosperity from the Lord is linked to rightness, righteousness, and salvation?

Did you happen to notice that prosperity from the Lord is linked to deliverance from whatever comes to attack or destroy us? My friends, that includes debt, disease, depression, maladies, even spirits. *Which means those things are the enemies of prosperity, and their presence can block or remove prosperity.*

    I repeat:
Deliverance from disease can facilitate the onset of prosperity.
    Deliverance from depression can facilitate the onset of prosperity.
    Deliverance from demonic oppression or possession can facilitate the onset of prosperity.
    Deliverance from sickness or generational curses can release prosperity to you.
    Which means all of those things can block or remove prosperity.

Are you catching on yet, that prosperity from the Lord means you are completely well, safe, abundant and blessed?

Are you seeing from God's perspective, that His brand of prosperity means you are well equipped to deal with anything and everything that comes your way, because you are stable, secure and equipped?

Christian, God's prosperity which includes His favor, empowers you in a unique and supernatural way.

Prosperity from the Lord is linked to being so self-sufficient that we have no lack, because nothing is missing.

Prosperity from the Lord is linked to having all our needs are met, and then some.

Prosperity from the Lord is linked to a personality and attitude that is pleasant and agreeable. And understandably so, because when your needs are met and you want for nothing, you enter in rest and joy!

Even in moments of temporary challenge or seeming difficulty, the joy remains because confidence in God's favor tells us breakthrough is on the way!

I realize I'm really driving this point home. Why am I emphasizing these definitions and realities regarding prosperity, so strongly? Because my friend, this is big. This is life-changing. Understanding the truth about prosperity can be a powerful game-changer *for you*.

Prior to reading those last paragraphs, if you had another understanding and perspective of prosperity, then someone lied to you.

Allow me to say that another way. If all of

the above is true (and it is) that means someone — either the devil, your history, society, or a false religious teaching, lied to you. Because as we have just seen: *Prosperity is of God.*

So then, why does Prosperity ruin so many people? Tough question, but let's answer it. The truth is, not everyone does well with wealth.

It may have to do with their upbringing, it may have to do with their nature, it may have to do with insecurity or irresponsibility. Whatever the reason, the unfortunate truth is that some people are irresponsible with money. Another unfortunately truth is that some people change when they get around money. In addition, some people change when they acquire wealth.

However, let's be clear: money itself is negative or positive, it is a neutral substance. Money itself is not the actual cause of wicked deeds or wickedness, even though it may be the tool used to facilitate wickedness.

Make no mistake, the same amount of money used to fund a drug trafficking business, can fund a children's hospital.
The same money used to produce pornography, can be used to produce Bibles.
Money can purchase hard liquor, or it can purchase food.

Money can be recklessly spent, or it can be wisely invested.

The very same money one person blows on foolish things, another individual can use to help the poor or sow into the Kingdom of God.

Money is not the problem: people's attitudes and intentions are.
Money as a substance is not the root of all evil, *the love of money, is.*

In the hands of a wicked person, money can do very wicked things. In the hands of a righteous man or woman, money can do lovely and wonderful things. It all depends on the orientation of the money-holder's soul.

One person may take a lump sum of money and use it to buy a house, support a ministry, provide for their children, bless other people, and store some up for their future.
Another person may take that same lump sum of money and blow it on drugs, inappropriate items, and foolish spending, helping no one, bringing glory to God in no way, serving no one but themselves and their own desires.

Again I say: money itself is a neutral currency that takes on the persona of the person whose hands hold it.

Therefore, it is written: *For the love of money is the root of all evil: which wile some coveted after, they have erred from the faith, and pierced themselves through with many sorrows.* - 2 Timothy 6:10

Some folks lose their humility and focus, in the presence of prosperity. Some become smitten with the things money can buy. Such people fall in love with the gift, and abandon the Giver.
Perhaps they don't realize it as it's happening. Perhaps caring friends, family members or even outsiders try to intervene when they see such an individual on the decline. But money has a way of warping the senses of the unstable and luring people into stilted thinking. Therefore, the Bible warns against the love of money, for good reason!

Another unfortunate truth is this: money has a way of luring believers into sin. It takes a sound mind, solid character, and unwavering devotion to the Lord, to withstand the temptation of an abundance of prosperity! This is why the Bible warns us about money's seductive powers, in that above quoted scripture, *1 Timothy 6:10.*

Satan is well aware of money's seductive power. That is why he uses it to corrupt influential people. Once those people are corrupted and deeply in love with money and all it can offer, those individuals are now able to be controlled. Have you not seen this, time and time again, in the media, art and entertainment industries, and in politics?

Sadly, such corruption has also occurred in the church. *And that is how prosperity got a bad name, in the body of Christ.* Irresponsible and corrupt leaders crashed and burned, sometimes publicly.

This sent a clear, unmistakable, but only partially correct message: *money leads to corruption!* A more accurate interpretation would have been: money *can* lead to corruption. It can, but it does not always, and it does not have to.

I have heard former church leaders express true remorse and repentance, at their own poor and damaging behaviors. Sadly, horrifically for the Lord and deliciously for Satan, the damage was already done. Every time a (former) leader fell or was exposed, the message went out loud and clear: Money is bad! Money ruins good people!

Some preachers became known as 'prosperity preachers'. To be honest, there are certainly more examples than I am comfortable with, of so-called men and women of God who have manipulated their congregations for personal financial gain.

However, not all prosperous congregations are abused, and not all prosperous preachers became so via dishonesty or manipulation. Some preachers became known as 'prosperity preachers' when in reality they were only teaching the *truth*, which is that God loves to bless and prosper His good and faithful children! Too late, the connotation was already there regarding prosperity. Too late, the message had already gone out that 'prosperity preaching' was fake. Thus, prosperity as a whole, gained a bad name.

Imagine the Lord's heartbreak, knowing some of His own formerly chosen, once anointed and trusted leaders, had fallen to the love of money. Imagine His heartbreak, knowing many now rejected His sacred provision, the gift of prosperity and favor, because of what a few bad apples had done.

But we learn from the Bible that God *will* allow us to make mistakes, even horrible ones. He does so in the hopes that we will learn, be humbled, glean a lesson, and turn back to Him. *-Luke 22:31-32*

As you go forth, reading and integrating the teachings in this book, I urge you to be in constant prayer that the Lord heal you of any discrepancies or sinful tendencies.

Pray the Lord prepares you to be a ready container for His prosperity.

Pray the Lord adjusts anything in you that needs adjusting, so you can step into His favor.

Pray the Lord reveals anything you need to do on your end, in order to facilitate stepping fully into the favor of the Lord.

Pray to have the faith, boldness, and readiness to step into God's magnificent and life-changing favor with a strong heart, a clear mind, and a right spirit!

My strong admonition to you is this, dear reader: keep your relationship with the Lord strong, and your humility high.

Keep your eyes ever focused on Christ!

As you commit more fully than you ever have to this Christian walk, you will go deeper into your relationship with the Lord and begin to encounter His precious gift of prosperity.

The responsibility will be yours to remember that this world is passing away. Your goal is to attain heaven. We are to store up treasures in heaven, not here on earth. - *Matthew 6:20*

The current assignment of the Church is to preach the gospel in preparation for the return of Christ eve as the Kingdom of God is made manifest.

Anything you receive or enjoy in the meantime, is temporary and must be regarded as such.

With this knowledge firmly in place, you will be ready to step into the favor of God!
For this is your Heavenly Father's provision and blessing for you, even as you await the return of our beloved Lord and Savior, Christ Jesus!
The favor of God is your *gift to enjoy…* in the meantime.
Read on.

Chapter Four
Poverty Is Satanic

As a child, I grew up very poor. I can clearly recall the times of plenty, and the times of lack. As I got older, I came to associate the 'plenty' with certain times of the month. Raised as the only child of a single parent, I routinely accompanied my mother to the offices of our local social services, where we sought financial assistance and public benefits as a way to supplement our income. Those monthly benefits allowed us to enjoy those 'times of plenty'.

I will never forget seeing my mother embarrassed and ashamed, as she was condescended to or accused of laziness by office workers, in exchange for a few public assistance dollars. Other social workers sometimes spoke to my mother with compassion or pity, but many regarded us with open disdain.

The treatment took a toll on my mother, of course. Her mentality and view of self-fueled her obsession with the pursuit of nice things. This caused little JoLynne to grow contemplative about the realities of our lives and the finer nuances of money, society, and status as they related to self worth.

From the time I was very small, I was introspective and spiritual, praying to God daily, somehow aware He was present and loved me, oddly aware I was called to some purpose that had yet to be revealed. Hence, these matters were of great interest to me. While I never broached the topic to my emotionally delicate mother, little JoLynne was making mental notes her entire childhood. I continued doing so into adulthood, when I would confront the issue of financial stability and solvency, for myself.

Our neighborhood had once been tidy and peaceful, or so my mother and aunties said. By the time I arrived however, it had become a mess — populated by drug dealers and broken down homes, unkept by often absentee landlords. Nightly sirens were a staple, and greatly increased in the summertime. Break-ins were common.

One of my favorite activities, anytime we went anywhere (we never owned a car until I went to middle school), was to look at houses outside of our neighborhood. Those houses fascinated me! I wondered who lived inside of them, how many children there were, if the parents were nice, whether or not they had a dog or a cat, and what they might be having for dinner.

I was dreaming of another life. I was making notes…

I was coming face to face with the inevitable and unavoidable dichotomy of life as we knew it, and I was marking it all down in my little mind.

You see, I was noting there was another way to live. And while I didn't fully realize it at the time, I was making plans.

At the age of eleven, I transferred from public school to private school, after obtaining a combination scholarship and financial aid. The improved environment afforded me a better education and a glimpse into 'how the other half lived'.

I made a few friends and was invited on playdates. Their homes were different than ours; their neighborhoods were different than ours. My friends' mothers behaved differently than mine, and their bedrooms looked differently than mine. Their closets were filled with toys and clothing that were definitely much different than what I had.

I was seeing the difference between poverty and affluence. I made more mental notes.

Soon, I began babysitting for a little pocket change. However, I was not allowed to keep my money, as it was needed for household expenses. Dutifully, I handed over all earnings to my mother. Sometimes she would allow me to keep a dollar or two.

Around grade eight, I also began working in the school office in exchange for tuition assistance. I didn't mind; while the other kids were going home or engaged in after school activities, I was obtaining clerical skills, conversing with adults, and teaching my babysitting charges to read or draw. This continued through high school.

By the time I reached college, I had come to the conclusion that no matter what it took, I would not be poor. I had no idea what the Bible said about poverty or generational curses. Therefore, I had no idea the uphill battle I'd have, to break the pattern.

Now, years later, I do understand the word of God. I understand that poverty enters and inhabits a bloodline, just as disease does. I understand that the curse of poverty can be maintained knowingly or unknowingly, or we can choose to break the curse. It's a choice we all have.

My mother never could break our curse. Like my grandmother, my mother died alone, single, poor. She never broke the curse. In spring of 2011, just months before my mother passed away, I made up my mind that I would be the one to end our curse.

In order to break the cyclic curse of generational poverty, a type of David must rise up on behalf of the family / bloodline, and slay the Giant. If no one does so, the Giant will continue to taunt, control, and terrorize the family.

Without a champion warrior to rise up and end kill the giant, the curse will continue, the pattern will continue.

Ultimately, someone must slay a family's personal Goliath, or that family will birth and raise new members who will assume the established lifestyle of poverty, believing it is normal.

The children may even come to believe poverty is something that cannot be overcome. They may believe, over time, that they're incapable or unworthy of living any other way.

Perhaps those children will someday long for a different life, a better life, like I did. But if they're not in possession of the knowledge or skills to slay the poverty giant, will they successfully break free? Perhaps, but maybe not. There are too many variables to say, for sure — the outcomes will be unique for each individual, depending on their personal circumstances and relationship with Jesus Christ.

I say all of this with confidence, because I have beheaded the giant called Generational

Poverty. I am the David of my family line. Many demons rose up to fight me, psychologically, supernaturally, and in the secular — but alas, the giant is dead.

I have eclipsed the annual income of everyone in my family line I have ever known. I am the first in my family to effectively plan legacy-level blessings for my children. Yet, I cannot assume any credit whatsoever for these feats; it was only through God that I was able to do so. - *Zechariah 4:6*

So yes, I have overcome generational poverty. I say this not to boast in any way, believe me. I tell you this only so you'll have confidence in everything I'm about to walk you through. In essence, I'm saying: *I know what I'm talking about; you can trust me.*

Having overcome that horrific generational curse, I have learned much about the giant called poverty. From being so near the beast for so long, I know its language, behavior, strategies, and weak points.

Please listen to what I'm about to say next, very carefully: *Poverty is Satanic.*

I believe poverty and cycles of poverty are curses that are Satanically generated and demonically sustained in order to keep people enslaved, in sin, dumbed down, disempowered.

Poverty is a Satanic strategy to incapacitate

you and make you unable to rise to your full potential and thus fulfill your destiny.

I realize I've just said a mouthful. Let's examine the clear evidence for this, in the Bible.

In *Luke 4:1-13*, we read the familiar story of Satan tempting Jesus in the desert. This story is revelatory in a profound way, because it shows us just how much influence Satan has in the earth realm at this time.

No, we are not ascribing more power to Satan than he is due. Rather, we are gaining truthful knowledge as to his position, so we can strategically defend and position ourselves!

In this Bible account, the devil approaches Jesus and immediately begins a tirade that climaxes with a mind-boggling offer. *Satan offers Jesus authority over all the kingdoms of the world.*

If Satan did not have the ability to give wealth and power to whomever he chooses, he would not have offered it. Furthermore, know this: if Satan can give wealth and power, he can also withhold it.

We learn from that account in the book of Luke that Satan is able to control and influence governments, corporations, global trends and initiatives, even the minds of believers. *- 2*

Corinthians 4:4

So let me say it again: Satan can give power and riches to whomever he chooses. This is the current (albeit temporary) world situation, as we anxiously and enthusiastically await the return of our precious Lord and Savior, Jesus Christ.

In the meantime, the devil is having a field day on the earth; causing wars, famines, corruption, death, and yes — poverty.

If the devil can give riches, he can also withhold them. If the devil can give power, he can also withhold empowerment.

We know Satan routinely influences the minds of individuals, and lures us into sin. We also know that God forgives our sinful natures, but active sin by choice, escorts us outside out God's will and thus out of blessing.

Grace and mercy are free and available to everyone. Salvation is free and available to everyone. We are no longer under the Mosaic Law; salvation cannot be earned by any ritual or offering. However, for the sake of staying true to the topic and goal of this book, allow me to gently state: that's not what we're talking about, here.

We're talking about how already saved and sanctified believers of Jesus Christ can step into the favor of God. I wrote *Stepping Into Favor* to help do just that—step into God's favor!

Doing so requires you to be in good standing with the Lord. Active and willful sin alienates you from the Lord. Hence, active and willful sin prevents you from stepping into God's favor. *And Satan knows it.*

Therefore, the devil deliberately attempts to lure you into active sin, knowing it will disqualify you from receiving God's favor.

The devil does not desire for you to be empowered, strong, clear, or blessed. A Christian in that state is dangerous!
A Christian that is empowered, strong, clear and blessed, is someone who can impact their community, testify to the Lord's faithfulness, create personal wealth.
A strong, empowered and prosperous Christian, can be a blessing to others!

A successful Christian who is walking in the favor of God, can be a World Changer and a Planet Shaker, because without the weight of poverty, they are free to do so! *And the devil knows it, so he seeks to bring poverty upon us.*

Poverty has a way of making people feel

defeated, even though they know they have the victory in Christ. Poverty has a way of making one feel unworthy, incapable. Poverty affects one's self esteem and confidence. Again, Satan knows this. So as a way of controlling people and hence keeping people dumbed down, the devil creates cycles of sin that induce or lead to poverty. Those same cycles of sin bring about generational curses, keeping families outside of the blessing.

Readers, it's a setup.
Poverty is Satanic.

However, the blood of Jesus allows us to break every chain! The blood of Jesus allows us to overturn the curse! The blood of Jesus turns a victim into a *victor!*

Thank God for the blood of Jesus, because by His stripes, we are healed — from every curse and infirmity, including the curse of poverty.

Allow me to show you just how powerful the blood of Jesus is:

The blood of Jesus remits sins.
- *Matthew 26:28*
The blood of Jesus saves us from wrath.
- *Romans 5:9*

The blood of Jesus grants us forgiveness of sin.
- *Colossians 1:14*
The blood of Jesus brings peace and reconciliation to God.
- *Colossians 1:20*
The blood of Jesus obtained eternal redemption for us.
- *Hebrews 9:12*
The blood of Jesus sanctifies us!
- *Hebrews 13:12*
The blood of Jesus is the means by which we overcome Satan!
- *Revelation 1:5, 7:14*
The blood of Jesus is the currency by which he purchased the church.
- *Acts 20:28*
Why?? How?? Because the LIFE is in the blood!
- *Leviticus 17:11*

The blood of Jesus is called the blood of the New Covenant and it is superior to anything Satan can derive or attack you with. Therefore, the blood of Jesus contains all the power required to overcome any and every generational curse!

Knowing that you have access to the Blood required to pull down the curse of poverty, is liberating. What is equally liberating is knowing that God has provided legal access to the timeless blessing of His favor.

In God's Word, the Holy Bible, the Lord has provided instructions for stepping into His favor. He has also lovingly informed us of exactly what we can expect to enjoy, once we step into the favor of God.

Are you ready to do so?
Goodbye, generational curses, it's time to access generational blessings!

It's time to step into favor!

Chapter Five
Favor Is God's Promise

Deuteronomy 28:1
If you fully obey the Lord your God and carefully follow all His commands I give you today, the Lord your God will set you high above all the nations of the earth.

In this opening verse, God is stating it plainly: if we fully obey Him, He will set us apart. But God doesn't simply say 'apart'; He uses the word *above* to indicate that due to His favor, we will be in an elevated position. Is this favoritism? Absolutely not; it is *favor,* brought on by our obedience.

Setting us high above means we won't be like the rest of the world. We will be in the world, but unlike others. We may live and work among people who do not love and obey the Lord, but we won't be like them. There will be something very different about us. A kind of favor will rest on our lives that will make unique, different, special. But note: in order to access this favor, we must *fully obey the Lord.*

Many Christians do not fully obey God, yet they wish to access the full favor of God. Many believers in Jesus do just that, they believe in him, but they don't follow him. Do you know someone like that? I see it all the time. Yet, this verse makes God's stipulation very plain: neither partial obedience nor full disobedience will give us access to the elevation that comes with the Lord's favor. It simply will not happen. God will not reward disobedience with favor.

I have seen God grant instances of favor in order to make Himself known to someone, and of course every sinner has access to the free gifts of salvation and grace. Favor, however, is reserved for the Lord's faithful children. Just as a human parent may reserve and grant certain privileges for the child who is respectful and obedient. Wow!

Where do you fall? Are you able to tap into the promise of this verse because you fully obey God? If not, you can start today. It isn't too late! There's a reason you're reading this, after all.

Some people pick and choose the commands and standards of God that suit them, and discard the rest. They obey the easy stuff, then find excuses for why they can't (won't) obey the challenging stuff. I call those folks 'Piccadilly Christians' because they 'pick and choose' what they like from the Bible, and ignore the rest. That kind of obedience is not obedience, at all. By God's standard, it is rebellion. Jesus even said, *But why do you call me 'Lord, Lord', and not do the things which I say?* Wow! Read more and learn God's perspective rebellion: - *1 Samuel 15:23, Proverbs 17:11, Ezekiel 20:8, Isaiah 1:19, 63:10*

Do not feel guilty, and close the book so soon. Do not feel condemned and think favor isn't for you. You *can* and you *will* access God's timeless blessing of favor, if you seek the Lord Jesus with all your heart in loving obedience!
- *Romans 8:1*

I promise, I am not here to guilt or shame you, but to help you shift into position so you can step into favor!

I want you to experience every good thing God can give you, and I want you to claim all the blessings God designed and designated for you since the beginning of the world! To do so, you must come into obedience. Make up your mind that obedience and favor is your portion, now. Commit your spirit to living God's way, so you can access God's favor. You will never regret it!

Sometimes people have a hard time submitting fully to the will of God because doing so would mean giving up sin. Perhaps their sin no longer feels like sin; perhaps they've come to view sinful habits as simply 'pleasures' or 'vices'. Yet if a behavior or practice is condemned in God's Word, it is sin — conversation closed.
Sin that becomes enjoyable, such as excess alcohol, pornography, recreational drug use and others, is called iniquity and it will block blessing.
- *Psalm 141:3-4*

Some popular and now societally accepted practices such as couples living together before marriage, having sex before marriage, regular alcohol consumption or socializing with unbelievers, have become acceptable to many

Christians.

Their relationship with Jesus is between them and the Lord. But it is my duty to point to the Word of God as our compass for right and wrong.

We cannot rely on our thoughts, opinions, or personal views to determine what is acceptable or unacceptable in the eyes of the Lord. And please remember, God always knows best! How many times have you made what you thought was a good decision at the time, only to regret it later? How many times have you acted in what you believed was good judgement or wisdom, only to have catastrophic or heartbreaking results? How many times would you have been better off… had you simply let God steer you?

It is best to let God lead us. He knows things about our biology, anatomy, psychology and spirituality that we don't and can't know, because He is our Designer, after all! - *Proverbs 3:5, Isaiah 55:8*

If we rebel against the full Word and Will of God, we are in disobedience. If we ignore some of God's commands because to obey them would infringe on our lifestyle or choices, we are in disobedience. This scripture in *Deuteronomy 28:1* leaves no room for misunderstanding.

Perhaps you've been walking in partial

disobedience or complete disobedience. I believe it's time to repent from that rebellion. God is faithful, and He is merciful. The Bible says that His mercies are new every morning. What a glorious supernatural provision! It's as though God knew humans need new mercy, each and every day! - *Lamentations 3:22-23*

My goal is to see every Christian obtain the full level of God's favor that is available to them!

If anything, I've written has made you uncomfortable, but has motivated you toward obedience and thus His favor, then I have succeeded! Glory to God!

Temporary discomfort in exchange for God's blessing is a palatable exchange! What a faithful and generous God you serve! Are you ready to do just that—are you ready to serve Him? Are you ready to exchange disobedience for obedience, now?

Any sin or rebellion you're currently in, is no surprise to God. Guess what? Sinners are true to their nature — we sin! Just as a dog barks and a cat meows, sinners inevitably sin. So, God has not given up on you, He has not rejected you, He stands ready to renew and bless you, now. Otherwise, you wouldn't be reading this book. Go ahead, smile. There is a very good chance

God arranged to have this book in your hands at the right time; what a loving God you have!

Your Heavenly Father has been watching… He knows where you've been.
He also hopes what you're reading will help turn your heart back to Him.

Again I ask, are you ready to do that?
Are you ready to repent and come into full obedience? If so, say this prayer aloud, right now:

Dear Lord, forgive me for my disobedience.
I seek You fully now, in Jesus' name.
My desire is to obey and love you fully now, and I declare so in Jesus' name!
Heavenly Father, I welcome Jesus into my heart anew, to be both my Savior and my Lord.
Washed clean in the precious blood of Jesus, I am now ready to serve you, Father.
As I seek Your face anew, see me, Father!
Look down from Heaven and see Your loving, obedient servant!
I ask for strength and wisdom to walk this path.
In Jesus name… AMEN.

Alright, let's continue.

Chapter Six
Obedience Is A Setup!

Deuteronomy 28:2
And all these blessings shall come on thee, and overtake thee, if thou shalt hearken unto the voice of the Lord thy God.

Wow! Obedience is a setup!
Obeying the Lord, hearkening unto His voice, sets you up for *FAVOR!*
My goodness, that's awesome!

Did you read what God just said in that above scripture? He said if you listen to Him (hearken unto His voice), the blessings He's about to itemize, will hit your life like a tidal wave of goodness.

In other words, if you obey the Lord, you step into His favor.

In other words, obedience is a setup!

That's quite an arrangement! God is promising to create a supernatural dispenser that releases favor to you continuously, according to His will for your current season.

God loves you that much?! Yes, He does. Not only is He parental in His love for us, but He knows we need continuous favor and blessing if we are to withstand the constant demonic onslaught that comes at us in this wicked world.

Please catch this: through the pages of this book, I am going to take you into a specific portion of the Bible wherein God reveals His wonderful provision, created specifically to bless us. The Lord seeks to relieve us of poverty, which we've already seen is a satanic attack. Christian, there are types of dysfunction that are now considered everyday life, things we cannot avoid as long as we are living in the world as it currently is.

What kind of daily dysfunction? Things we now consider normal or at least common, such as rude cashiers, road rage, gangs and drug wars, child abuse, infidelity, discrimination, bondages such as human trafficking, on and on.

When King Jesus returns, those things will be done away with. Glory to God! But until then, while we use every precious moment to tell others about salvation through Christ Jesus, we can also walk in the blessing and covering of the Lord. This is our gift from God, our Christian heritage. Hallelujah!

God's love for you as His child, is parental. He sees us as His kids.

God, like most parents, has rules and guidelines. Many parents establish 'house rules' they expect their children to respect and adhere to. As a mother, some of my house rules require my children to keep their bedrooms clean and tidy up the kitchen after themselves.

When children get older, a parent may

require them to adhere to a curfew and other rules such as prioritizing or organizing their time. Parents set these type of rules because they love their children and want the best for them. Those parents have experience and wisdom the children don't yet have. In most cases, the parents also want to teach their children good habits, discipline, and protect them from the destruction that comes from poor habits and behaviors.

Even if a child doesn't fully understand the need to brush their teeth daily or launder their clothes regularly, an attentive parent will require the child to follow those rules, because good parents know and want what's best for their child.

When children get older, the rules change, but there are still rules. Wise parents usually advise teens to steer clear of the wrong crowd and never text while driving. The teen may not like or particularly enjoy those rules, but they're incredibly wise rules nevertheless, and act as a safeguard.

Is a parent mean, strict, or disconnected from current times simply because they impose rules and guidelines? It may seem so to the child, but the parent knows someday that child will understand and perhaps even thank them.

It's the same way with God.

Some people feel God is an absentee tyrant who only wants to restrict us and boss people around. Not so. Each and every guideline set forth in the Bible, is structured to benefit us, keep us from harm, steer us in the right direction, and bless us.

God knows that without His guidelines as our protection, we are susceptible to so much worldly danger! The Bible says Satan walks around like a roaring lion, seeking to devour us. - *1 Peter 5:8*

God, on the other hand, seeks to protect us. He also seeks to bless us. Because like any good parent, the Lord loves to see His obedient children happy and living well.

When we abandon God's way of doing things, we literally come out from under His umbrella of protection. - *Deuteronomy 30:19*

When a child deliberately disregards a parent's rules, the parent is then left no choice but to deliberately withhold blessing. What parent rewards a rebellious, disobedient child? No one I know!
It is the same with God.
But when we obey Him, He releases a level of favor that actually *pursues us*.
When we obey Him, we are empowered to step into His favor.

Let's read *Deuteronomy 28:2*, again:
And all these blessings shall come on thee, and overtake thee, if thou shalt hearken unto the voice of the Lord thy God.

One of the greatest gifts God has given you, is your free will. For better or worse, God allows you to make your own decisions. The God who made you, this earth, and the entire universe, will never force you to have a relationship with Him.

He loves you though, and every single day, God is hoping you'll come to Him.

Just like any good dad, the Lord wants to bless you.

Just like any good dad, the moment you begin to cultivate a good relationship with your Heavenly Father, He will begin blessing your life with favor.

According to this verse of scripture, the level of favor and blessing the Lord reserves for those who are consistently obedient to Him, is aggressive! That type of favor actually tracks you down, invades your life, and impacts every area of your existence!

I don't know about you, but that's the kind of favor I want!

Let's continue.
We've only gotten started.
Now that we know obedience is a setup for blessing and favor, let's go deeper!

Chapter Seven
Favor Wherever You Go

Deuteronomy 28:3
Blessed shall you be in the city, and blessed shall you be in the country.

Once you step into God's favor, only disobedience can cause you to step out of it. Changing geographical locations cannot take you outside of God's favor. Moving from the city to the country, cannot take you outside of God's favor. Moving from the suburbs to a downtown loft, cannot remove you from the favor of God.

Once you step into God's favor through full obedience to the Lord, it's yours no matter where you go!

Picture the favor of God as a spotlight. Wherever you step, the spotlight follows you. Wherever you go, the spotlight shines on you!

If you step into a forest, the spotlight follows you. When you get into your car, there's the spotlight illuminating you. When you go into the doctor's office, court room or banker's office, that spotlight is with you!

God's favor will follow you wherever you go. Glory to God! What a comfort! What a provision!

Christian, before you enter into any situation, pray the favor of God over yourself. When you rise each morning, praise the Lord for waking you up, praise Him for all the blessings you currently have, and ask Him for more favor!

When favor is your portion, it accompanies you throughout your life! Tell God you claim and receive His favor, each and every day. During trying or difficult times, pray the favor of God over yourself and loved ones, like a shield. - *Psalm 5:12*

But that's not all. Not only will the Lord extend the benefit of His favor to you regardless of your current location, but He will bless the things attached to you. Let's look at the next part of this passage.

Chapter Eight
Favor And Blessing For Your Children

Deuteronomy 28:4
Blessed shall be the fruit of your body, the produce of your ground and the increase of your cattle and the offspring of your flocks.

This means your children will be blessed. What excellent news for parents! This is particularly hopeful news for those whose children are living outside of the Lord, or not yet saved.

Perhaps your children have not yet accepted Jesus, maybe they're living in sin. Pray the favor of *Deuteronomy 28:4* over your offspring, that the Lord may extend mercy and grace to them. Ask God for the time required, and for a Holy Spirit awakening to come to those children! If the spirit of Jesus can awaken former Saul of Tarsus and transform him into the esteemed Apostle Paul, Jesus can affect and save anyone!

When you have time, I encourage you to read the entire stirring account in *Acts chapter 9*, as it is very encouraging and inspiring!

I also encourage you to plead the blood of Jesus over your unsaved or wayward children. 'Pleading the blood' is when you stand on the authority of Jesus though his life-saving blood, as shown in *Luke 10:19 and John 14:12.*

1 John 1:7 says it this way: *But if we walk in the light as He is in the list, we have fellowship with one another, <u>and the blood of Jesus Christ His Son cleanses us from all sin</u>.*

The blood of Jesus eradicated the need for animal sacrifices, forever.

The blood of Jesus is the new covenant by which we are reconciled unto God, and saved from eternal death.

It is the blood of Jesus that provided the final, perfect sacrifice.

It is the blood of Jesus through which we attain forgiveness for our sins.

The blood of Jesus is the supernatural cleansing agent by which we are made clean.
- *Hebrews 10:1-18*

There is great supernatural power in the sinless, perfect blood of Jesus! Pleading that supernatural power over your unsaved or sinful children, then, is impactful in ways we cannot fully fathom!

Finally, I encourage you to also pray *Ezekiel 22:30* over your unsaved or sinful children.

That scripture reads: *Ezekiel 22:30: So I sought for a man among them who would make a wall, and stay in the gap before Me on behalf of the land, that I should not destroy it…*

This is where the term 'standing in the gap' comes from. It means to literally stand before God in prayer or travail, appealing to the Lord on behalf of a sinner. In this way, unbelievers or sinners may obtain mercy.

As a believer, you may entreat the Lord for time or opportunity, you may ask the Lord to grant the unbeliever mercy from His wrath or even the effects of their own sinful behavior.

What a wonderful provision by which Christians may 'stand in the gap' on behalf of our love ones who are not yet saved or are currently not in good standing with the Lord.

You may have heard it said that someone was protected, healed or blessed, because, for example, they had a praying mother or grandmother. This is the very principal we're talking about. We're talking about the Lord extending time, patience, mercy, even blessing — *to an unbeliever who is deserving of judgement.*
In many cases, a sinner will not reap what they sowed, because a believer in good standing 'stood in the gap', in that delicate but powerful place between them and the Lord, and made intercession for them.

The Bible tells us the fervent, effectual prayers of the righteous, availeth much. We also know we are to make prayerful intercession for one another, regularly. - *James 5:16, 1 Timothy 2:1*
Even the Holy Spirit makes prayerful intercession on our behalf! - *Romans 8:26*.
So intercession and prayer for one another

is a powerful tool. Glory to God! What a loving Heavenly Father we serve!

But as good as this is and as grateful as we are, this is not what *Deuteronomy 28:4* is talking about.

This verse details a remarkable provision by which the Lord allows the favor of a believer in good standing, to also bless that believer's children. Mercy and grace are precious, but this verse is talking about *favor*.

Once again, all I can say is, Glory to God! I know there have been times my own favor has been extended to my children, who were rebellious at the time.

I am eternally grateful for that grace upon my beloved babies.

I am equally eager for my children to experience God's favor for themselves.

Extension of your favor to your children, cannot and will not compare to them receiving God's favor for themselves. It will be ideal for those children to access God's timeless blessings, for themselves. That certainly is God's wish, as He wants all people to be saved and come unto knowledge of the truth! - *1 Timothy 2:4*

How life changing and truly wonderful it will be for your unsaved children to experience the fullness of God's favor for themselves!

Let's continue, now.
Again, we've only scratched the surface.
If you're ready to gain further understanding of God's favor and how it will impact and bless your life, turn the page.

Chapter Nine
He Blesses Your Efforts!

Deuteronomy 28:5
Blessed shall be your basket and your kneading bowl.

This scripture has very special and powerful significance, as the Lord once again reveals Himself as Jehovah Jireh, our Provider.

From the beginning to the end of our lives, He is our Source.
Not man.
Not a job.
Not a program.
Not any of those things — because God can facilitate, cancel, override, or arrange any of those things, or something completely different, at any time. In the course of your walk under the favor of the Lord, you will see Him do so! God is going to do things for you that will be mind boggling, quite literally!

Just as God provided the sacrificial ram to Abraham in place of Isaac, just as the Lord provided manna to the freshly liberated Israelites, He will provide for your needs.
Just as Jesus provided an ample buffet of fish and loaves to thousands of hungry souls, your Lord is going to provide for you.
- Genesis 22:14, Exodus 16:12, Matthew 14:13-21.

That's who He is.
He is Jehovah Jireh, your Provider.
He is Jehovah Jireh, your Source.

He is Jesus, the one who came and tore the veil so you can have access, abundance, forgiveness, reconciliation, restoration, prosperity. Jesus got the job done as the final sacrifice so you can have it all!

From Him flows not just manna and quail, but milk and honey.
From Him flows not just adequate provision, but ample provision.
From Him flows not just enough, but plenty.

It is very important that you read and fully integrate what I am about to say, next: God wants to provide for you, but He doesn't want to give you just enough; He wants to give you *more than enough*.

How do we know? Because He says so:

Ephesians 3:20 ~ Now to Him who is able to do exceedingly abundantly above all that we ask or think, according to the power that word in us…

Philippians 4:19 ~ And my God shall supply all your need according to His riches in glory by Christ Jesus.

Matthew 6:33 ~ But seek first the kingdom of God and His righteousness, and all these things shall be added to you.

Christian, these are the Scriptures you

hear other Christians quote often, because these are the power-house verses we need to stand on. When the trials of life come, we need to confidently go to the Lord in prayer and plead these verses over our situation. According to His will, the Lord will respond by granting you favor, because His Word does not return void! - *Isaiah 55:11*

In the model prayer found at *Matthew 6:5-9*, Jesus taught us to acknowledge the Lord's provision, daily. Christian, this is powerful as it helps prevent us from ever becoming too caught up in the rat-race or pursuit of provision.

In other words, the model prayer helps us keep our work and secular employment, in perspective — because at the end of it all, God is our Source. *He* is the one who provides, who can provide, and who will provide!

While the Lord desires us to work for our keep because He loathes a sluggard (lazy person, see *Proverbs 6:6*), He also makes it crystal clear lest anyone forget: from Him all blessings flow.

Throughout the Scriptures, God's consistent message to us is: love Me, choose Me, serve Me, and I will be your ever-loving Heavenly Father who provides for your needs and so much more.

He says it to us over and over again — too many scriptures for me to cite.
Love Me.
Choose Me.
Serve Me.
Do this and I will be your ever-loving Heavenly Father who provides for your needs and so much more.

Let's look carefully at *Deuteronomy 28:5*, because this verse is both powerful and very telling.

When the Lord says your basket and kneading bowl shall be blessed, that means He is going to bless what you *gather and/or create*.

You cannot gather something you haven't planted or initiated. You cannot gather what you haven't sown. So, this verse is not talking about a gift or sudden outpouring from God, it's talking specifically about the Lord *blessing the work of your hands*.

My daughter loves to make bread. Through trial and error, she's become pretty good at it! I don't eat much bread due to dietary choices, but the bread she bakes, I will eat! If she ever decided to go into business making and selling that bread, I have no doubt the girl would be a success!

She would succeed because she is taking a passion and monetizing it.

She would succeed because she is taking a skill at which she excels, and turning it into a service that can benefit and nourish others.

She would succeed because her bread is really different. (Nope, I'm not sharing the recipe!)

But so too would she succeed, perhaps above and beyond anything she ever imagined, because as a young lady who loves the Lord, she would be well within her legal rights to ask God to bless her little bread business according to Deuteronomy 28:5.

She could also *request success* by legally asking the Lord to bless her basket, which refers to her materials, ingredients, tools, etc.—BUT A BASKET IS ALSO—the vessel used to gather or reap a harvest. Therefore, by blessing the basket, God is blessing you with the resources required to create the harvest!

My daughter could also request that her kneading bowl be blessed, which of course is the place where the work takes place, where the creative stuff happens, where the service/offering/goods are prepared.

Now that I think about it, perhaps I'll encourage my daughter to start a little business! When God blesses a little business, it often doesn't stay little for very long! Why? Because according to this verse, the Lord is willing to bless it!

But this scripture applies to so much more than baking and cooking.
You may apply this verse to every creative or business effort.

To make this verse personal for you, digest this: *Deuteronomy 28:5* says God is willing to bless what you put effort into creating, planting, starting, making.

Furthermore, if you want to create, plant or start something, God will provide the resources to do so. The Lord will bless the basket which refers to your supplies, resources and harvest; so too will He bless the kneading bowl, which refers to your creative or production process.

Whatever your career, work or business, I encourage you to stand on this scripture and ask God to bless your business! I encourage you to entreat His favor in this area!
If you start a foundation or community based effort that is in harmony with Scriptural principals, you may ask the Lord to bless it!

God is a do-er.
He's also a creative genius.
We see evidence of His doings and master creativity when we simply look around us. Consider the universe and our beautiful earth, teeming with life, scientific wonders and magnificent artistry!
Now catch this: God celebrates and blesses the very same attributes in His children.

Deuteronomy 8:18a says: And you shall remember the Lord your God, for it is He who gives you power to get wealth...

Each individual is created with specific attributes and characteristics, abilities and highly individualized penchants and skills. Those things combine to form a unique skill-set or 'tool box' that belongs to you, alone. When we utilize the 'tools' God has placed in our 'tool box', so often we discover ways to obtain personal wealth.

Utilizing our God-given skills for the purpose of creating wealth, generational blessing and family legacy, is part of God's will for us.
What's more, God promises to bless those efforts.

To God be the glory!

STEPPING INTO FAVOR

Chapter Ten

His Safety Shall Surround You Like A Shield

Deuteronomy 28:6
Blessed shall you be when you come in, and blessed shall you be when you go out.

Traveling Mercies.
Angelic escort.
Protection on the road.
Protection in your home.
Protection from attacks by the devil.
Protection from other wicked humans.
Protection from anything that is against God's will for your life.
Protection as you leave home or travel somewhere, and protection as you make your way back home.

I wish I had time to share all the stories I personally know of, where people have been protected as they went about their way.

I know of people who've been protected in an accident, protected during home invasion, protected from the destructive wiles and attacks of the enemy as they traveled or simply as they conducted ordinary daily affairs.

I've heard stories where a person's Bible somehow shielded a gun shot.
I've heard stories where a person's fervent effectual prayer protected them in what surely should have been a life-threatening car accident.

I've known people who were alerted to a weapon forming against them in the spiritual realm, allowing them to protect themselves through intercessory prayer.

- Isaiah 54:17, James 5:6b

God looks out for His own, according to His will for their lives!

In this scripture, God promises to look out for you, as you go about your business.

Do plead the blood of Jesus over yourself every time you leave the house.

Do pray for traveling mercies every time you embark on a trip.

And *do* stand on this scripture in order to walk in God's protection from harm, daily!

How do you stand on it? By remaining fully obedient to the Lord, then reading it aloud and declaring it over your life, in Jesus' name!

In *Ecclesiastes 9:11*, wise King Solomon emphasized that accidents and unexpected happenings befall us all.

But make no mistake, Solomon's father, wise King David also emphasized that the Lord's favor surrounds us like a shield!
- Psalm 5:12

Chapter Eleven
His Favor Shall Protect You From Your Enemies

Deuteronomy 28:7
The Lord will cause your enemies who rise against you to be defeated before your face; they shall come out against you one way and flee before you seven ways.

Wow! This is serious!

Actually, as we study the scriptures, we learn that God takes your enemies very seriously. We can describe His protectiveness over you as parental. Like any good parent, the Lord is quite concerned when someone unjustly attacks or antagonizes you. To that end, God vows to address your enemies on your behalf.

We need a *Selah* moment after those statements. I want you to let the gravity of that information sink in.

God is concerned about your enemies, and He vows to address them on your behalf—*wow!*

Earlier in the Bible, we get acquainted with the Lord's solemn standard when it comes to engaging your enemies.

Consider *Exodus 23:20-22* ~ *Behold, I send an Angel before you to keep you in the way and to bring you into the place which I have prepared. Beware of Him and obey His voice; do not provoke Him, for He will not pardon your transgressions; for My name is in Him.*
But if you indeed obey His voice and do all that I speak, then I will be an enemy to your enemies and an adversary to your adversary.

Again, a very solemn revelation as to the nature and habit of the Lord regarding His people.

The Israelites had every reason to take the Lord their God seriously; they'd already seen His handiwork when it came to dealing with Pharaoh! In *Exodus chapters 7 through 12* inclusively, we read how the Lord sent warnings, demands, and finally attacks on the Egyptian Pharaoh, in the form of 10 plagues.

Each plague was highly personal to Pharaoh, because each plague targeted a different Egyptian god. In this way, the Lord was making an open mockery of the Egyptians' pagan gods.

The One True God meant to leave no doubt in anyone's mind that He was in charge, He was in control, and there was no one above Him.

God attacked the Egyptians with blood, frogs, lice, flies, pestilence against the wild-life, boils, hail, locust, darkness — and finally the Lord launched the plague of plagues, the very weapon Herod would later use to try and murder baby King Jesus: death of the first born.

Let me say it this way: *God sees your enemies as His enemies.*

The Israelites had suffered at the hands of the Egyptians, now it was time for supernatural recompense.

By the end of it all, Pharaoh knew exactly who he was dealing with — the Lord of Lords, the One True God, the Maker of heaven and earth!

The Israelites' enemy became God's enemy, and lives were altered forever!

Later in 2 Chronicles chapter 20, we see the Lord intervening once again on behalf of the Israelites, aiding them to defeat the people of Ammon, Moab, Mount Seir, and later, others.

From these accounts, we derive the prayerful decree that is also our battle cry:
The battle belongs to the Lord. - 2 Chronicles 20:15.

One of the ways God still blesses His faithful servants, is by fighting for them. Walking in the favor of God means having the confidence in the Lord as your Defender.

He is that, and more.

The Lord will not only defeat your enemies for you, but he will cause them to be *defeated before your face.*

That means you will see their defeat. You will be aware of the battle, aware of your vindication, aware that the Lord is addressing the matter for you. Glory to God! It is not enough that the Lord will fight for you; He wants you to know it, so you can give Him the glory He deserves when you get the victory!

In *Psalm 3*, King David wrote of his experience when fleeing from his own destructive son, Absalom. David wrote: *Lord, how they have increased who trouble me! Many are they who rise up against me. Many are they who say of me, There is no help for him in God. But You, O Lord, are a shield for me, my glory and the One who lifts up my head. I cried to the Lord with my voice, and He heard me from His holy hill. - Psalm 3:1-4*

Later in *Psalm 23:5*, we see the Lord's standard of protecting His own and fighting our battles, again:
You prepare a table before me in the presence of my enemies; You anoint my head with oil; My cup runs over. Surely goodness and mercy shall follow me all the days of my life; and I will dwell in the house of the Lord forever.

God sees every attack on your life. He sees when Satan attacks you, and He sees when the devil uses people to attack you. The Lord sees and notes every unfair situation you endure. He sees, from His Lofty Throne on high, every battle you walk through, and every enemy who comes against you. Because you are faithful and loyal to the Lord, your God promises to address these situations for you.

His promise is this: your enemies may attack you one way, but they'll be so sorry they did, they will flee from you seven ways. That means they won't be able to exit your vicinity quickly enough! In short, they'll be sorry they ever attacked you.

Not only will they be sorry, but they will have to watch you be blessed, as part of their payment. That's what God means when He says He will prepare a table before you in the presence of your enemies. - *Psalm 23:5*

Imagine a buffet table, arranged just for you. On that table are your favorite foods, the spoils of your success, evidence of the blessing on your life. Now imagine the people who have hated and harmed you the most, watching as you enjoy everything on that table. They may not partake of the buffet, it's for you. They may not look away, God is making sure they see.

Isaiah 54:17 promises: No weapon formed against you shall prosper, And every tongue which rises against you in judgement You shall condemn. This is the heritage of the servants of the Lord, And their righteousness is from Me, says the Lord.

Note the part that says, ...*this is the heritage of the servants of the Lord.*

In other words, protection from your God is your birthright, your blessing.

Protection is your portion!

This is simply part of the provision freely

given by your loving Abba Daddy.

I'll say it again: protection is your birthright.
Supernatural protection is your birthright. Vindication before your enemies, is your birthright. This is the heritage of the servants of the Lord! This is one of the benefits of God's favor! Hallelujah!

Chapter Twelve
He Will Bless Your Acquisitions, Holdings, And Pursuits

Deuteronomy 28:8
The Lord will command the blessing on you in your storehouses and in all to which you set your hand, and He will bless you in the land which the Lord your God is giving you.

Shall we go a little deeper? *Deuteronomy 28:8* contains a hefty promise; and while they're all hefty in this chapter, this verse bears in depth examination.

So far, we've observed specific aspects of God's personality as revealed in His promises. We've gotten a glimpse of *who He is*. We know Jesus the Son of God as revealed to us through the books of the Gospel, Matthew, Mark, Luke and John. Now we're learning the personality and character attributes of The Father. Of course they are one, but from studying the entire Bible we see specific attributes that are revenant to these facets or manifestations of God.

The Bible says God is the same yesterday, today, and forever, so we can rely on the Lord's attributes never changing. - *Hebrews 13:8*
In an ever-changing world of volatile people, this is quite comforting.

In *Genesis 12:1*, we find God issuing quite a promise to Abraham, the promise of land and legacy, for generations to come. The very scriptures we've been studying thus far in *Deuteronomy 28* demonstrate the Lord's clear love for family and His desire to bless your family.

Now, *Deuteronomy 28:8* reveals God's promise to bless your acquisitions and holdings, *as well as* the lands He will add to your holdings.

A storehouse is only required when your life has become so bountiful and blessed, that you have holdings. A storehouse is only required when your harvest is exceedingly abundantly great, or when you must *store* your abundant acquisitions.

Christian, God is interested in blessing you at the level of personal legacy. He wants you to provide not just enough for yourself, but for others. He is interested in providing for you not only for this season, but the next, and the next, and the next.

Your God is a God of legacy!
Your God desires you to have storehouses, fruitful work, and land.

I realize this kind of teaching disturbs the individuals who are convinced Christians are meant to live simply and even suffer. Nevertheless, this teaching is directly from the Word of God, so let's be clear: choosing to live simply or in a state of consistent suffering, is a choice.

I realize that statement may offend Christian brothers and sisters who live in impoverished countries where the cultivation of personal wealth is particularly difficult. I cannot speak to their situation, but I will say I believe

God crafts a destiny for each of us, according to Jeremiah 1:5. Am I saying it is some people's destiny to suffer? Not at all, because the promise of God's favor is available to us all at any time!

There are some things that will remain a mystery to us, until we get to heaven and greater understanding is made available. There are many injustices in the world that will persist until King Jesus returns and shuts it all down.

Until then, I encourage you to stand on the promises of God found in the Holy Bible. I encourage you to pray for the less fortunate ones.

And I encourage you to receive this truthful statement: you are not here to simply survive, but to thrive. Every scriptural verse we have studied thus far, has shown this.

Could it be some of us are destined to step into favor specifically so we can help the less fortunate? Could it be that the cultivation of wealth among the body of Christ is part of God's plan to battle the attacks of the devil on the impoverished? Of course, this is true.

As you begin to step into God's favor and experience the wonderful blessing of the Lord's prosperity at greater and greater levels, I encourage you to pray and ask God this vital question: *What do you want me to do with this prosperity, Lord?* Some of you are going to be given resources, land, finances, influence, etc. — specifically so you can be a blessing to others. Amen.

Now let's continue studying this verse.

In *Deuteronomy 28:8*, we learn the favor of God also covers what you acquire, own, have. We learn the favor of God extends as a covering and blessing on all you put your hand to, which means your work and pursuits as they align with the Lord's will. Furthermore, we learn that God desires what you acquire, own or have, to not only be abundant enough to require a storehouse, but to include *land*.

As a child, we never owned a house. All my young life, my mother rented apartments. Twice, because she so desired an actual house of her own, my mother recklessly rented single houses, but we were evicted both times because we simply couldn't afford it.

Some of those rentals were nicer than others, but all of them were rentals. Home ownership was something that felt out of reach for my mother, and for good reason — she simply didn't have the means or the credit. She also didn't have the mentality or acumen.

Mom never saw herself as a homeowner, not truly — otherwise she would have pursued it, fiercely. Mom never believed she could position herself properly and thereby set herself up for home ownership, otherwise she would have pursued it.

Catch this: some of us do not own homes because we do not have home ownership mentality. We may want a home, but deep down we don't believe we can have a home.

We may desire it, we may even feel desperate for our own home, but until we believe we are worthy, able and deserving, it probably won't happen.

If it does happen, it's questionable whether or not such a person will be able to keep, maintain and sustain the home, because they are not in possession of the manner of thinking and lifestyle required to steward it.

Am I being negative? Not at all — the Bible says it plainly:
As a man thinketh in his heart, so is he. - Proverbs 23:7

Our thoughts impact our lives. And too often, our thoughts dictate our lives.

In *Matthew 21:22* after explaining the lesson of the withered fig tree which explain the power of having thoughts without doubt, Jesus showed us that if we believe, we will receive. *That* is how powerful our thoughts are!

The same mentality my mother had, imposed itself on me. Up until the time I had my second child, I too rented apartments but never owned a home. Up until my son was nearly finished with high school, I did not have financial independence. I was unstable financially, and did not have my own home, just like my mother.

There is an instability and unspoken sense of transience that comes with renting but never owning. I'm not talking about the individuals who choose to rent, for personal reasons. To be fair, some folks prefer renting in order to maintain the freedom to leave or change situations, with ease. To be fair, due to marital or employment circumstances, some people may prefer the less committal lifestyle of renting.

However, some of us desire to put down roots. Some of us truly want to create stability and cultivate equity. For those, renting becomes an albatross. Instability and transience can become not just a lifestyle, but something much worse: these things can become a mindset.

Renting also puts one at the mercy of a landlord. Too many times to count, my mother and I were evicted or asked to leave with only the required legal notice, which was usually 30 days but sometimes less.

In addition, a landlord may increase rent, suddenly. A landlord may or may not keep the property in good repair. A landlord may or may not honor the rental agreement, and if the tenant is dependent on that dwelling as their only option for a living arrangement, the situation can become abusive. I have lived it and seen it countless times, therefore I can say with authority: a tenant is at the mercy of the landlord, and not every landlord is fair or kind.

Listen, there is no shame in renting. My job within the pages of this book is to simply explain some of the manifestations of the favor of the Lord, *so you are informed and empowered!* The Bible makes it clear that your God is a God of legacy and legacy building. He desires for you to have and own a home, if you want it.

The Bible describes us as children of God, utilizing some very powerful terms. The Bible says as God's kids, we are more than a conqueror, we are the head and not the tail, we are born to lend and not borrow, we are co-heirs with Christ. There is a level of independence, blessing and personal empowerment that comes with being a property owner. If you desire to own property but currently do not, go to the Lord and ask for His favor in this regard! Stand on *Deuteronomy 28:8* as your supporting scripture!

As we've already learned, disadvantage and poverty are Satanically driven and demonically maintained. This chapter is not meant to disrespect or offend anyone who is currently renting. Yet again I'll say: if you desire to have a home on land of your own, go to the Lord in prayer and entreat Him for that blessing!

But please, Christian, do the following things, as well.
Ask God to prepare you for home ownership. Ask Him to help you position yourself mentally. Ask Him to shift whatever mindsets need shifting, so you can prosper. Ask God to assist you financially so that you are able to step into home ownership.

God is well able to help with your details. He owns the earth; that means He owns the banks! Since the Lord literally made human beings, He is able to influence all people! Never say home ownership is out of reach; for Jesus said all things are possible with God!
- *Matthew 19:26*

Perhaps you worry, as my mother did, about being able to handle the responsibility of owning a home. Perhaps your past reveals a pattern of financial irresponsibility. Ask God to help you with those matters.

Pray to the Lord about further transforming you by the renewing of your mind. Pray for wisdom, discernment, and a ready nature. God is faithful to meet you where you are and work all things together for your good! - *Romans 12:2, 8:28.*

Once you acquire anything — be it funds, resources, a home, land, a business (to name a few of the common acquisitions), the favor of the Lord will command a blessing on those things.

God will bless all you put your hand to — family, homemaking efforts, job, career, business pursuit, ministry, destiny and purpose.

If you desire to acquire land for any of those things, ask!
If you want these things and you're willing to be made ready, ask God!
His Word makes it clear He desires them for you.

Chapter Thirteen

There Is Power In Consecration And Obedience

Deuteronomy 28:9
The Lord will establish you as a holy people to Himself, just as He has sworn to you, if you keep the commandments of the Lord your God and walk in His ways.

Ah yes, holiness. God is holy; therefore, He requires us to be holy.

If we're being honest, holiness is what many Christians struggle with, the most. At times the presence of sin can become habitual, as we've already discussed. At times, habitual sin can become enjoyable, then it becomes iniquity and iniquity presents the danger of the formation of a curse.

The temptation to sin can be quite severe. Especially when the world and all its' systems promote sin as 'normal'.

According to many in the music, entertainment and art industries, common behaviors include promiscuity, immodest dress, fornication, homosexuality, along with adultery and infidelity. Someone in the television industry told me that some of these things occur so frequently, they are considered completely normal. This individual said such behaviors are seen simply as part of life. When they occur, they are minimized if not completely overlooked, because it's 'normal'.

The Lord urges us as Christians to separate ourselves from the ways of the world. Just because we must live and function in this world as it presently is, doesn't mean we have to subscribe to its' ways.

The Bible says although we are in the world, we are not to be part of it, nor should we love the things of the world. - *1 John 2:15-17*

The Bible also describes a time when people would be lovers of themselves, covetous, boasters, proud, blasphemers, disobedient to parents, unthankful and unholy. - *2 Timothy 3:2* The next verses describe those people as being without self-control, despisers of good, lovers of pleasure rather than lovers of God.

We are instructed to go into all the world with the gospel of Jesus Christ, but that doesn't mean we need to join ourselves to the protocols and lifestyles of non-Christians. - *Mark 16:15*

Let's be real. Some Christians have a hard time separating themselves from the way of the world. They 'push the envelope' as I like to put it, in their style of dress, the music they listen to, the films and shows they watch, even their associations and habits. - *1 Corinthians 15:33*

This whole *Go into all the world* assignment, known as the Great Commission, requires discipline and discernment!

It also requires a healthy balance. For we do not want to be so far removed that we are unrelate able. Yet the Bible makes it clear that we are to stand out, not blend in.

1 John 2:15 says ~ Do not love the world or the things in the world. If anyone loves the world, the love of the Father is not in him.

1 Peter 2:9 says ~ But you are a chosen generation, a royal priesthood, a holy nation, His own special people, that you may proclaim the praises of Him who calls you out of darkness into His marvelous light…

Blending in too much, puts you in danger of encountering situations that may compromise your holiness. Pushing the envelope too much puts you in danger of violating God's standard of holiness.
Listen, God doesn't expect you to be perfect — He knows that's impossible. We're all sinners, deserving of destruction, saved by the grace and love of God through Christ Jesus.

Nevertheless, God requires you to choose and maintain a holy lifestyle, as His child.
If you desire to step into favor, I encourage you to cultivate personal holiness, then attempt entreating the Lord for favor.

I'm not saying non-Christians aren't good people; I know plenty of non-Christians who are great people! Many of those folks are kind, giving, thoughtful, even spiritual. But if they are not saved by grace, washed by the Blood, having received salvation through Christ Jesus alone, they are not destined to inherit the Kingdom of God.

Good and caring people fornicate and engage in other sins. Sweet and thoughtful people worship false gods. Generous and good-hearted folk who profess to love Jesus, also engage in lifestyles God calls unholy.

Each of these groups have one thing in common: unless they repent of all sin and receive salvation through Jesus Christ, those individuals will not inherit the Kingdom of God, they're destined for an eternity in hell.

God will not tolerate sin, and He will never bless sin.
In order to step into His glorious favor, you must remove all known sin from your life.
Removing known sin will make you holy in God's eyes, to the best of your human ability.
Choosing a lifestyle of holiness, qualifies you for God's favor.
Choosing to live holy to the very best of your ability, allows you to access the timeless blessings of God!
See: *Revelation 22:15, 1 Corinthians 6:9-10, Galatians 5:19-21, Ephesians 5:5*

This is tough stuff to talk about, I realize that. These are the 'pills' that are hard for unbelievers to swallow, because quite frankly, humans are born with an Adamic (sinful) nature, therefore we don't want to live holy! We've been pre-programmed for unholiness! Complicating matters, many of us have acquired a taste for sin over the course of a lifetime!

But those tastes will escort us straight to hell if we do not remove them from our lives.

Again, tough stuff to discuss, but in order to shift you into position to receive God's favor, we need to discuss it.
See: *Romans 5:12, 1 Corinthians 15:21*

Reader, I'd like to ask you a question. If you have been unable to access the favor of God, could the presence of sin be the reason?

I am not judging you, please know that. Again, we are *all* sinners, saved only by grace! - *Ephesians 2:8*

I want to help you. I want you to step into favor and walk in that favor! So therefore Christian, the question remains: could sin be what is blocking you? Could sin be the reason you have not fully stepped into the favor of the Lord?

You don't ever have to tell me, to be honest it's none of my business.

But please be honest with yourself.

It is time to position yourself properly. It is time to empower yourself to step into God's favor!

1 Thessalonians 4:7 ~ For God did not call us to uncleanness, but in holiness.

1 Peter 1:13-16 ~ Therefore, gird up the loins of your mind, be sober, and rest your hope fully upon the grace that is to be brought to you at the revelation of Jesus Christ; as obedient children, not conforming yourselves to the former lusts, as in your ignorance; but as He who called you is holy, you also be holy in all your conduct, because it is written, Be holy, for I am holy.

See also Leviticus 11:44-45

Hebrews 12:14 ~ Pursue peace with all people, and holiness, without which no one will see the Lord…

The Bible is clear. God is holy; therefore, He requires us to be holy. Consecration is the act or process of making something holy. Therefore, to remove sin from your life means you are consecrating yourself. Personal consecration is something every Christian must strive for, and do their best to maintain.

This is not easy, so make it easier to do by separating yourself from the world, that is, individuals who do not desire to serve Jesus and live holy.

Is it possible to live without sin, fully? Until the day we die, we will all sin and fall short of the glory of God. But we must try to please our Lord! Especially if we are to have the confidence and stance required to ask for His favor. - *Romans 3:23*

Hear me well, reader: God needs to see you trying. He needs to see you striving to be obedient.
Pursue consecration.
Pursue a holy lifestyle.
Doing so will empower you to step into the favor of God!

Do not let this 'conversation' overwhelm, intimidate or discourage you. Let it motivate you! God will never ask you to do something that is impossible! His grace is sufficient to strengthen and fuel you during your pursuit of holiness!

After all, greater is He who is in you, than He who is in the world! You can do all things through Christ, and with God nothing is impossible!
- *2 Corinthians 12:9, 1 John 4:4,*

STEPPING INTO FAVOR

Matthew 19:26, Philippians 4:13

Be encouraged. There is power in consecration and obedience.

Some people think consecration takes away ones' power because you're giving up a lot, but it's the opposite. You are gaining so much by choosing holiness! The only thing you're really giving up is a one-way ticket to hell!

There is power in living holy!
There is also privilege.
That privilege is called *God's Favor!*

Chapter Fourteen

You're About To Step Into Fear-Inspiring Favor!

Deuteronomy 28:10
Then all peoples of the earth shall see that you are called by the name of the Lord, and they shall be afraid of you.

This verse leaves little to the imagination and even less to conjecture, but let's break it down anyway!

Notice your God says it directly and simply: the favor that's coming into your life is going to make people drop their jaws.

People are going to see there's something special about you, you have the true power of the Living God with you, and that's going to cause two things to happen.

First, people are going to know God loves you and has your back, because you belong to Him. Second, they're going to be afraid of you. There's simply going to know that it isn't a good idea to mess with you!

Reason being, when you come to a fight, you don't come alone; you bring with you the clout and raw power of the Lord! You bring the loving and generous favor of the Lord. That favor follows you everywhere you go!

Christian, walking with the Lord is powerful! Stepping into favor and living under that canopy of blessing, is powerful!
Having the Lord's hand continually on your life, even when it doesn't look or feel like it, is powerful!

Knowing that at the end of the day, all things are going to work together for your good, is powerful!

Having full assurance that the Lord will provide all your needs simply because you are seeking first His Kingdom and righteousness, is quite frankly, a game-changer! It saves you from stressing the way others do. It saves you from worrying, which is the equivalent of praying for what you *don't* want. Having full assurance that the Lord's favor covers you, gives you peace of mind and confidence of spirit. Praise God!

You can now walk forth into any situation, any storm, against any odds, knowing your powerful God stands beside you.
You can now rest in knowing your provision will not be mere scraps but an abundance according to all God's riches.
God's favor is not only powerful all by itself, but it is empowering for your life.

And that kind of supernatural power translates to fear and intimidation to some onlookers.

Many are going to see there's something different about you. They're going to notice you walk in protection, peace, provision! You're going to walk in joy, faith, hope!

Any and all who look your way will notice you have a confidence and prosperity about you, that cannot be bought or attained through any other means except by God Himself!

And that, my friend, is going to scare the pants off of some people!

Your enemies are now God's enemies. *Yikes!* No weapon formed against you will prosper. *Yowza!*

The Lord is going to give you strategies to create wealth and provision for yourself and your family. *Whoa!*

You're going to have access to the Gifts of the Spirit, which may allow you to produce words of knowledge or prophecy, be the vessel through which God works miraculous healings, and much more — to God be the glory! And when the world sees these things, they will marvel at the God you serve! For your God is a formidable force not to be toyed with!

What glorious provision the Lord has created for you. In this Satanic world of war and violence, the promise of God's favor is a source of great comfort and strength. In this world of wickedness and evil doers, you can now rest in God, knowing that He's got your back. I encourage you to give Him praise, right now!

You don't have to be afraid anymore, Christian. Stepping into favor means you can walk in boldness, confidence, peace.

Other religions claim their gods have power. Of course, no religion but Christianity is the correct path to God, because only Jesus saves and Jesus is the only way to the Father. - *2 Timothy 1:9, John 3:16*

The Bible reveals the truth about those other gods: they are false. Unable to speak, see, hear or smell — they're capable of absolutely nothing, devoid of any life or power. - *Psalm 115:4-8*

We learn from the Holy Bible, which is the highest authority on the planet, there is no other God besides our God and that no one comes to the Father except through His Son, Jesus Christ. - *Isaiah 45:5, John 14:6*

Thank goodness you have Jesus!
Thank goodness you have access to everlasting life through him!
And thank goodness for the Lord's incredible, marvelous, life-changing favor!

Let's continue.

Chapter Fifteen
Supernatural Increase Of Holdings And Children

Deuteronomy 28:11
And the Lord will grant you plenty of goods, in the fruit of your body, in the increase of your livestock, and in the produce of your ground, in the land of which the Lord swore to your fathers to give you.

This verse is multi-faceted and it is powerful. As we continue forth, embracing the relevance of these verses for our personal walk with the Lord, let us remind ourselves of the truth found at *2 Timothy 3:16 ~ All Scripture is given by inspiration of God, and is profitable for doctrine, for reproof, for correction, for instruction in righteousness.*

To which I say, Amen!

This verse emphasizes the Lord's loyalty and the worth of His word. Deuteronomy 28:11 will bless everyone who reads it, but it will especially bless those who are ready to establish themselves and prosper.

Here, God makes it clear that a tangible sign of His blessing will the increase of your children, family, possessions and holdings.

This part of the verse is especially powerful for those who are striving to build or rebuild themselves. Perhaps you are just starting out, seeking to set up house. Perhaps you're coming out of a period of struggle or financial ruin, and desire to create a prosperous life.

As I was studying this verse, I couldn't help but think how powerful this promise can be for married couples struggling with infertility or anything to do with child-bearing.

If that is you, I encourage you to go to the Lord in prayer and stand on this Scripture. Respectfully approach the Lord and with humility and boldness, and request that He fulfill this scripture on your behalf. Request God's favor in helping you bear a child! Be sure to point out that you are an obedient and loyal child of His. The following verses are also relevant.

Psalm 34:17 ~ *The righteous cry, and the Lord hearth, and delivereth them out of all their troubles.*

Proverbs 15:29 ~ *The Lord is far from the wicked but He heareth the prayer of the righteous.*

But *Deuteronomy 28:11* doesn't stop there. The Lord also promises to increase your livestock and the produce of your ground.

Is this verse only intended, then, for farmers? Absolutely not! But if you happen to be a farmer or have a penchant for gardening, this is an excellent verse to declare over your increase!

The Lord has given us this earth and all manner of self-seeding foods. He has provided animals from which many derive food, goods and labor. Because the Lord sees these things as gifts and resources with which you may sustain and prosper yourself and your household, He has promised to increase these things.

If you are a landowner or farmer with livestock, I encourage you to declare this scripture over your animals. Entreat the Lord to fulfill His promises by multiplying your livestock!

Perhaps like me, you aspire to grow your own food. Maybe you've already begun. When you begin to plant, declare this scripture over your garden or crops, no matter how large or small! The Lord is faithful to give the increase!

This verse can help keep your garden or crops safe from pests, storms, intruders, and more.

The Lord is, after all, Jehovah Jireh your Provider and as such, He takes your sustenance quite seriously!

What a gift it is to have such a good Father!

Chapter Sixteen
Abundantly Prosperous And Debt Free

Deuteronomy 28:12

The Lord will open to you His good treasure, the heavens, to give the rain to your land in its season, and to bless all the work of your hand. You shall lend to many nations, but you shall not borrow.

What a powerful verse! In it, the Lord is clearly showing His never-changing intention toward us: He desires us to thrive and prosper. He does not want us beholden or indebted to others. The Lord is also clarifying just how powerful and literal His hand can be in our lives.

Here, God is saying: *I am able to open My heavenly treasure to you, and I will do it. I am able to establish you to the extent that you are debt-free.*

This verse emphasizes that the Lord will cause your lands to prosper by sending life-giving rain. He will do so according to its season, note that. In other words, we must not expect rain, 'round the clock. It will not rain—literally or figuratively, without ceasing. *There is a season for rain* — please catch that. It's because there must also be seasons of cultivation, growth, harvest, and rest — according to His will for your life.

So as God orchestrates and oversees the seasons of your life, He will provide rain in its season, helping you to grow, assisting you to create your future harvest. Glory to God, what a marvelous provision!

In the Bible, 'rain' characterizes the Lord's blessing. In agriculture, without rain, crops do not grow. Without crops, our Biblical ancestors would not have been able to eat. How important, then, was rain? *Very.*

So, in a very literal sense, God will give *the life-supplying provision that will make the difference between eating and starving, between success and failure.*

This applies to farmers and gardeners, today. If you currently farm or garden, stand on this scripture and entreat the Lord for blessing and favor over your crops!

Again, rain symbolizes the Lord's blessing.

Ezekiel 34:26 says: And I will make them and the places round about My hill a blessing, and I will cause the shower to come down in their season; there shall be showers of blessing.

So then, outpouring from the Lord means He is blessing us with life-giving substances: resources, finances, provision. 'Rain' can mean providing you with whatever you require.

I once knew a woman who had not yet developed sound financial stewardship. She had two young children, and very little money. She stood in grave need. She and her children had recently relocated to a new city in an attempt to start anew. Unfortunately, she'd been forced to leave the majority of her belongings behind. All she'd been able to take with her was what she could fit in their vehicle: their clothing items and a few other essentials.

How would she furnish the small apartment she'd been able to procure for her small family? What would they do for furniture, kitchen items, towels? She did not know. The woman was a new born again believer, currently developing her relationship with Jesus and a supporter of my ministry.

She began putting in job applications immediately, and connected with a local church. Right away, she began volunteering for various duties at the church. During the day, she would search for a job and care for her children, as they settled into their new apartment.

Within days, members of the congregation rallied and began showing up on her doorstep with bags and boxes full to overflowing, with home goods.

Almost overnight, the woman had every single thing she needed, and then some! The provision was exceedingly, abundantly above all she could think or imagine! She received so much, she didn't know what to do with the excess! She received things she wanted, but never expected to get!

That, my friend, is what happens when the Lord opens His heavenly treasure to you!

What did that woman experience? The favor of God. A season of *rain!* The Lord saw her efforts, and blessed her. Soon, she did find employment, and she is prospering to this day.

Friend, the Lord wants to do the same for *you.* He wants to open the windows of heaven and pour out a blessing on your life! God wants you to step into His favor!

Now let's look at the part of the verse that says God will bless *all* the work of your hand. That three-letter word 'all' is key; it means no effort or job is too meager for God to notice and bless.

In other words, do not think your current job is too insignificant for God to pour His favor out upon it. Additionally, do not let any temporary or transitional occupation be so insignificant *to you* that you do not request and receive the Lord's favor upon it! The scripture says He'll bless *all* the work of your hand — and doing a good job where you currently are, will most assuredly set you up for a future promotion!

I encourage you to request and receive favor wherever you are, even in the low places as you make your way to the high places!

As we've already established from the Word of God, the Lord looks at a person's willingness to work, as it is an indicator of one's character and ethic. Sure, perhaps your employment status is meager, currently. But when the Lord takes note of your positive attitude, good work ethic and loyalty to Him, you never know what His favor will soon bring you!

Now let's take a look at the latter part of the verse. *You shall lend to many nations, but you shall not borrow.* God wants to pour out His favor, His good treasure, on your lands and work so abundantly that the result is Biblical prosperity, which includes financial independence.

God's will is for you to be empowered to lend to many others, but never have to borrow. *That* is the extent to which the Lord wants you to experience and receive His favor! Glory to God!

When we choose to work, using the abilities, talents and capabilities God has given us, He will bless those efforts.

Some people reading this chapter may feel convicted, because they have not been a hard worker, haven't given the Lord something to bless, or cannot work. Those are three separate categories of people; allow me to address them individually.

To those who need to improve their work ethic, I would say: if you are healthy and able, do so! I'm glad you feel convicted, because the

Lord most certainly does not support or respect laziness. Perhaps it's no coincidence that you're reading this; perhaps this is the Lord's wake up call to you! He loves you and believes in your potential so much, He's speaking life into you right now, motivating you to action! If you know you need to improve your work ethic, commit to doing so. There's nothing stopping you. When you do, this scripture can then apply to you!

When the verse says God will bless the work of your hand, that clearly shows you must have something to present to Him, something to 'put on the altar', so to speak. If you have been lazy or not motivated in the area of work, I speak encouragement over you now in the name of Jesus!

I believe this can be the beginning of a new season in your life! A season in which you grow and step into the Lord's favor like never before! Please read *Proverbs 6:6,9 and 2 Thessalonians 3:10*.

To those who feel they have not yet 'given' the Lord something significant to bless, again I call your attention to the fact that God will bless *all* the work of your hands. If you're a stay at home mom, God will bless your mothering and homemaking! If you're a restaurant worker, the Lord will give you favor in that setting!

If you're a student trying to find your way or a middle-aged person trying to restart your life, God will give you favor right where you are. As long as you are working and trying, in good standing with the Lord, you can and you shall step into His glorious and abundant favor! Believe it and receive it, my friend!

And finally, to those who cannot work, I have a word for you as well. The Lord has provision for those who are disabled, elderly or ill. God knows your situation! He is concerned with the condition of your heart and the depth of your love for Jesus. Do you love the Lord? Study the Bible? Do you attend church to the extent that you are able? Are you loving and kind to others? In true instances where people cannot work the Lord provides.

> *Psalm 68:10 ~ The Lord provides for the poor.*
> *James 1:27 ~ The church should be looking after widows and orphans.*
> *Proverbs 28:27 ~ There is a blessing for those who help the poor.*
> *Luke 6:38 ~ As Christians, we should be motivated to assist the needy.*
> *Deuteronomy 15:7-8 ~ It is our sacred obligation to help our brothers and sisters in Christ who are in need.*
> *See also: James 1:27, Proverbs 21:13, Galatians 2:10*

All of the above scriptures are incredibly stirring and very clear, but I cannot close this part of the chapter without sharing the following:

Proverbs 19:7 ~ He who is gracious to a poor man lends to the Lord, and He will repay him for his good deed.

1 John 3:17-18 ~ But whoever has the world's goods, and sees his brother in need and closes his heart against him, how does the love of God abide in him? Little children, let us not love with word or with tongue, but indeed and truth.

From these verses above, we learn that one very powerful way God provides for the needy and impoverished, *is through us*. That's what it means for God to make you a blessing to others. Often, Christians are prospered specifically for this purpose! God will read the condition of your heart and hence know that you can be trusted as a carrier of supernatural wealth, because according to the condition of your heart, God knows you will freely aid and assist others!

Let us move on.

The Lord may choose any number of ways to prosper you and free you from debt. He will do the choosing; your job is to simply posture yourself for the blessing!

He may release sudden windfalls and gifts. I have seen God move heaven and earth to bless one of His children by surprise, according to His will.

Now let's look at the latter meaning of *Deuteronomy 28:12*. The Lord makes it very clear here that He does not wish us to live in debt. Debt is bondage. All bondage brings a lack of freedom and fear. Those are not God's wishes for you. Further on in that same chapter in Ezekiel we just read from, the Lord says some very stirring things:

Ezekiel 34: 27-28: Then the trees of the field shall yield their fruit, and the earth shall yield her increase. They shall be safe in their land; and they shall know that I am the Lord, when I have broken the bands of their yoke and delivered them from the hand of those who enslaved them.
And they shall no longer be a prey for the nations, nor shall beasts of the land devour them; but they shall dwell safely, and no one shall make them afraid.

Friends, that says it all. Debt makes you vulnerable. It empowers others to prey on you, quite literally. In this current system of things, it is often necessary for people to finance their homes, cars, and other purchases, thus placing them in debt. Doing so is not a bad thing, but let's be clear: if God has His way in your life, you will receive the favor and provision required to liberate yourself from debt!

Do you believe that is possible? God says it is! Can you imagine living a debt-free life? God says you must!

You are destined to lend, and not borrow.
You will help others, but no longer need to ask for help.

This is one of the most poignant blessings of the favor of the Lord.
Thank you, Lord!

Chapter Seventeen
Strong, Free, Empowered --- That's You!

Deuteronomy 28:13
And the Lord will make you the head and not the tail; you shall be above only, and not beneath, if you heed the commandments of the Lord your God, which I commanded you today, and are careful to observe them.

Strength! Liberation! Freedom! Empowerment! These things are the heritage of the children of the Lord when we walk under the glory and blessing of His favor!

No longer will any past discrimination, abuse, or instances where you were condescended to, be your portion. God is going to make you the head and not the tail! That means you will walk in confidence. You will know who you are in Christ Jesus. God seeks to empower you!

No movement or societal organization can give you true freedom or empowerment. No organization or movement can give you favor. It's impossible; true freedom, empowerment and favor can only come from your Creator!

If you are aligned an organization or movement that takes your focus away from the Kingdom of God to any degree, I encourage you to cease all interaction. Cut your ties. A man or woman cannot have two masters. Our focus must not be split. God wants all of you!
- *Matthew 6:24*

I strongly entreat you to align yourself with the Lord your God *only*, not the thoughts, passions or issues of man. Such things are passing away and will never bring true peace and restoration to the earth — only King Jesus can do that.

Truth is, earthly organizations and movements, no matter how passionate or justified they may be, are of the flesh; they are carnal. We are called to be of the Spirit, aligned only with the heart and will of the Father. *- 2 Corinthians 10:5*

Our cultural heritage or biology of origin must never take precedence over our *true heritage*. *We are Christians, born again into the family of God!*

Reader, may I share something personal with you? People ask me my ethnicity all the time. I'm aware I'm a tough species to figure out! My response is the same each and every time: *I am a child of God!*

When I was washed in the blood, I became a new creature in Christ!
When I was born again into the Kingdom of God, I became a citizen of His royal court!
My alliance is to Jesus and the Kingdom alone, no ethnicity or organization of man!

The Bible says those who come to Jesus are *all* children of God — there is no exclusion. Thank the Lord we can *all* come freely, leaving former identities and affiliations behind!
- John 3:3-8, Galatians 3:26

Some people feel a loyalty to their culture or homeland; that's understandable. But as a Christian, we are instructed to become one, not divided.
Our God calls for unity, not cultural division!

Jesus said: *If a kingdom is divided against itself, that kingdom cannot stand. And if a house is divided against itself, that house cannot stand.* - Mark 3:24-25

Strength, freedom and empowerment comes from being unified, not divided.

Remember this, always: The Lord always seeks to add to you, and to multiply you.
It is the devil who seeks to subtract from your life and divide the body of Christ. Amen.

Christian, this may be hard to hear, but I love you enough to say it: if there is division or split loyalty in your heart, whether known or unknown, you may be inadvertently blocking God's favor. For the Lord does not support division of any kind.

I urge you to release division of all kinds.
I beg of you to remove all worldly alliances from your life. Give your heart and focus to King Jesus, only.
You will be so grateful that you did!

Doing so will align you with the spirit and method of God, thereby moving you into position to receive His glorious favor. Hallelujah!

The Bible says in *Psalm 92:12* ~ *The righteous shall flourish like the palm tree; he shall grow like a cedar of Lebanon. Those planted in the house of the Lord shall flourish in the courts of our God.*

Your Lord seeks to strengthen, liberate and empower you, fully. God wants you to flourish and grow. He wants to see you firmly planted and thriving!

I am so excited for you to step into favor! My friend, it's going to change your life.
Do you believe it? If so, lift up your voice and claim your favor today!

Chapter Eighteen

God Expects Your Loyalty In Return

Deuteronomy 28:14
So you shall not turn aside from any of the words which I command you this day, to the right or the left, to go after other gods to serve them.

In His infinite love and mercy, the Lord wraps up this stirring discourse on favor in the twenty-eighth chapter of Deuteronomy by telling us very plainly: He expects our loyalty.

We are not to stray to other gods. We are not to mix-and-match our spirituality. We are not to become lax in our pursuit of the Lord. At all times, we are to keep ourselves pure and unblemished, before the Lord — by keeping our eyes on Jesus, alone.

All those who practice divination, which is seeking information about the future from a soothsayer, along with spirit mediums and witches, are condemned and rejected by the Lord. The Bible also includes sorcerers and those who interpret omens. These things are detestable, abominations to the Lord. - *Deuteronomy 18:9-12a*

Christian, as a lover and follower of Christ Jesus, you must remain as loyal to your Heavenly Father as you want Him to be to you.

No other brands of spirituality. No divination. No astrology. No seemingly harmless practices such as angel cards or yoga, because these things are rooted in false religion and the occult.

The occult is governed and empowered by none other than Satan himself. The Bible reveals that the devil is about to disguise himself as an angel of light. - *2 Corinthians 11:14*

This is one of the reasons Satan is called the great deceiver, the one who deceived the whole world. - *Revelation 12:9*

This knowledge helps us to understand why God is so very strict regarding this statute. We are never, ever, to go after other gods, nor are we to serve them.

Some people have a hard time believing their spiritual practice is of the devil, because it seems so harmless, peaceful, and brings them such enjoyment, such a soothing feeling.
Again, Satan is skillfully deceptive on a supernatural level; it is folly to think humans can discern for ourselves. It is better to trust God, who knows all things! Why play with your future? Why risk going to hell?

Exodus 20:3 is very clear: *Thou shalt have no other gods before me.*

Jesus himself warned: *Many will say to me in that day, Lord, Lord, have we not prophesied in thy name? And in thy name have cast out devils? And in thy name done many wonderful works? And then I will profess unto them, I never knew you' depart from me, ye that work iniquity.*

Christian, what a sobering passage. There are those who will believe they were following Jesus, even serving Jesus, even doing great works in his name and for the Kingdom of God. Yet in the end, they're in for a rude awakening.

We find a crucial piece of information in the last four words Jesus spoke in that passage: *ye that work iniquity.*

Let's gain an accurate understand of exactly what iniquity is; most know it's sin, but it is every-day, run of the mill sin? Not at all.

Psalm 141:3-4 says: Set a guard, O Lord, over my mouth; keep watch over the door of my lips. Do not incline my heart to any evil thing, to practice wicked works with men who work iniquity; and do not let me eat of their delicacies.

The word 'delicacies' reveals much. Another translation uses the word 'dainties'. This reveals that some sin is *enjoyable*. As you know, Christian, things that are enjoyable can become *desirable*. Once something is desirable, it can become habitual. And once it's a habit, as the saying goes, habits are hard to break.

So then, iniquity is the type of sin that the person comes to view as enjoyable. They may realize it is sin, but now they've come to enjoy it.

The etymology of this verse also reveals much. Upon research, we learn that iniquity refers to sin that tastes sweet while being enjoyed or can give us some type of advantage.

Take care, Christian. Iniquity is lethal! Becoming a slave to iniquity can lead you straight to hell. While living, this enslavement will block you from God's favor. Wouldn't you agree that is just too steep a price to pay?

Come out of iniquity, now! Salvation through Christ Jesus awaits you! Forgiveness by grace awaits you! Beyond that, a lifetime of walking in the favor and blessing of the Lord awaits you!

Choose life and favor, over sin and iniquity! No iniquity, no matter how temporarily enjoyable, is worth trading the favor of God and life eternal, for!

The God who created you wants you undivided devotion. He desires to see you living holy and in obedience to Him. In return, He promises to rain down His glorious favor upon you, bringing blessing and prosperity into your fold! What a glorious promise!

Chapter Nineteen

Step Into Favor And Stay There!

Joshua 1:8
This Book of the Law shall not depart from your mouth, but you shall meditate in it day and night, that you may observe to do according to all that is written in it. For then you will make your way prosperous, and then you will have good success.

Now that you are equipped to step into favor, I encourage you to do so, and stay there! Take care to remain loyal to the Lord. If you slip into sin or make a mistake, repent quickly. The Lord is faithful to forgive you if your heart is contrite and true!

1 John 1:9 says: If we confess our sins, He is faithful and just to forgive us our sins, and to cleanse us from all unrighteousness.

Psalm 51:17 says: ... a broken and contrite heart, O God, thou wilt not despise.

Do not let any sin keep you from the favor of God! Friend, it's never worth it—never. Do not be ashamed or afraid to go to your Heavenly Father. Let the scriptures above assure you that when we are truly sorry and repentant, God will forgive us.

Perhaps you're in sin, right now. You want to lay hold of the promises in this book, but don't know if you can. You want to step into favor, but you're not sure if God will accept you. Again, I say unto you dear Christian, walk away from the sin, and Jesus will cleanse you. Turn *away* from the sin, turn *to* Jesus.

Running to Jesus and giving him your burdens, is all you must do. Do so, right now. Take hold of Jesus' strong hand and never let go!

- *Matthew 11:28*

The devil will tell you you're too far gone, that God will never take you back. The devil is a liar! The Bible says Satan lies so much, that lying is his native language! God reveals the truth about Satan: there is literally no truth in him! - *John 8:44*

Why would Satan tell you the truth when he wants you to fail? Why would the devil tell you anything that's true about your life, when his goal is to acquire you as a citizen in hell, one more soul for him to torture and torment?

Your adversary the devil who wants you to feel ashamed, condemned. But your Bible tells you there is no condemnation in Christ Jesus! - *Romans 8:1*

The devil is a liar. You are *not* too far gone. God loves you, He wants you, Jesus can and *will* wash you clean. Once you come to Jesus and give your heart to Christ, you *will* step into the favor of God, regardless of what any rogue punk devil tries to tell you! Rebuke that liar! - *James 4:7*

Favor is your portion.
It is your birthright.
Do not allow any sin or any devil's lie keep you from living the life of victory, wellness,

prosperity and joy that are rightfully yours! Jesus died to make all this available to you!

Step into favor and stay there!
I have faith that you can, and I'm praying for you! I have faith that you will, and I'm celebrating with you!

I know many who will read this book, came out of poverty, like myself. Maybe you're in poverty, right now. Guess what? You are not going to stay there!

Many who will read this book, began to believe the cycles and patterns of their family, would be their cycle and pattern, too. Guess what? Not so. I'm so glad you now know that simply isn't true!

Now you know what God intends for you.
Now you know the life you dreamed of, is possible.

Wellness, good health, safety, security, freedom, abundance, success, financial blessing and generational legacy is not only within your reach, but it is your right as a child of the Most High God!

Congratulations — you're about to step into favor! Life will never be the same. You're about to live in such a way that will bring glory to your God and testify as to who He is.

You're about to eclipse every lie the devil ever told you about your financial ability. You're about to overcome every generational curse of poverty that ever tried to come upon you!

This is your season, this is your time!
Never will you forget this life changing experience of stepping into the Lord's favor!

Glory to God!

Chapter Twenty

A Special Message From JoLynne Whittaker

Thank you so much for reading Stepping Into Favor. I pray this revelation from the Word of God makes a deep, deep impact on your life. I pray you are now empowered and motivated to step into favor!

I know what it's like to live without the favor of God, and I know what it is like to live with it. I prefer favor, always! Walking in the favor of God does not promise everything will always go our way or that we'll get everything we want. Favor promises our God is always with us, always fighting for us, always looking out for our best interest.

Favor promises that good things are in store, because God always seeks to increase us with what is best for our lives.

Favor promises you'll receive not just what you need, but more than enough, even some of the secret desires of your heart. What a promise! What a God!

Stepping into favor means the Lord will shield you from your enemies, lead you into victory, and bless us according to His will for our lives—*without ceasing.* Favor doesn't go away. It isn't like a faucet that turns on and off; as long as you are in good standing with the Lord, saved and sanctified, the Lord's favor will be there.

I encourage you to stay close to Jesus. Let him be both your Savior and your Lord. That means your salvation is secure through Christ Jesus, *and* you obey his words and commands. This is how you will stay in favor!

Favor in the valley, favor on the mountain-top!

There will inevitably be times when God is silent. That does not He has retracted His favor; sometimes God is simply working quietly. Other times when it seems quiet, the Lord may be allowing certain things to culminate or play out.

Do not let the quiet times siphon your faith. The word siphon when used as a verb, means to draw out, to take away from. So, what I'm saying is, do not let the times when God seems silent, detract from your faith. Do not let those times cause you to question the Lord. Stay in faith at all times! Trust that your God is at work, preparing connections and opportunities, working out solutions for you.

Stepping into favor means you *know* an outpouring is coming! Stepping into favor gives you the security that, no matter what conditions look like now, soon those clouds are going to be heavy with rain!

You may not know exactly when your outpouring is coming, and you may not know how, but because your God is faithful and you walk in the Lord's favor, you know *He will* show up right on time! - *1 Corinthians 1:9*

When things go quiet… that usually means God is up to something!

The quiet times are usually when God is working behind the scenes. He has already assigned His holy angels to you, decrees have been made in the heavens, now you are simply waiting for the Lord's favor to come to fruition. Do not grow impatient, stay in faith! For you shall reap if you do not grow weary! Those who wait upon the Lord renew their strength, mount up with wings like eagles, run and not be weary, walk and not faint! - *Galatians 6:9, Isaiah 40:31*

If you do your part, love Jesus with all your heart and remain in good standing as a Christian, God will do *His* part and show up with the favor! For God is not a man that He should lie; He promised His favor and the Lord always delivers!

In the midst of your attack, declare Favor!

Spiritual attacks are inevitable, even as you walk in favor. The Bible informs us of the devil's three-part agenda: to steal, kill, and destroy. That agenda never changes; therefore you must expect the devil to target any and every area of your life with that agenda. - *John 10:10*

While God is a constructive force, the devil is a destructive force. Be wise and be prepared for the inevitable attacks. I've often said being a Christian can be equated to walking around with a target on your back, because the devil targets us as followers of Jesus Christ. But the excellent news is that God has given you a powerful suit of armor!

The Bible says in *Ephesians 6:11-18: Put on the whole armor of God, that you may be able to stand against the wiles of the devil.*
For we do not wrestle against flesh and blood, but against principalities, against powers, against the rulers

of the darkness of this age, against spiritual hosts of wickedness in the heavenly places. Therefore take up the whole armor of God, that you may be able to withstand in the evil day, and having done all, to stand.

Stand therefore, having girded your waist with truth, having put on the breastplate of righteousness, and having shod your feet with the preparation of the gospel of peace; above all, taking the shield of faith with which you will be able to quench all the fiery darts of the wicked one. And take the helmet of salvation, and the sword of the Spirit, which is the word of God; praying always with all prayer and supplication in the Spirit, being watchful to this end with all perseverance and supplication for all the saints...

Your God is powerful and His Word is a mighty defender!

I have encountered many spiritual attacks and I can tell you with complete gratitude and truth, it was the Word of God and the Favor of God, that kept me. God is faithful and He is mighty!

The Word is powerful! Learn to declare it! That's exactly what Jesus did when the devil attacked him. Each and every attack was refuted with a Bible verse! - *Luke 4:5-13*

Favor is powerful! For God shows us time and time again, He is faithful to protect and shield His beloved children according to His will for their lives.

In the midst of your attack, declare the Word! Declare Favor! Speak life and know that your victory is guaranteed, for Jesus already won the ultimate Victory at Calvary!
- 1 Corinthians 15:58

Don't Forget To Stand On The Word

Christian, don't forget to stand on the Word. That means if God said it, *it must come to pass* — because He is just and true, because He will not allow His Word to return void. If you are in good standing with the Lord, submitted to Christ Jesus and consecrated unto the Lord in a holy sin-free lifestyle, you can and should go to God in prayer and decree His Words over your life! That's what it means to stand on God's Word.

If you need favor in a particular area of your life, go straight to your Holy Bible and *find a scripture* that speaks of blessing or breakthrough in your particular area. Call out to your God and ask Him to honor that Word for you. Trust that He will do it. Trust in His timing, His method, His delivery. I say again, our God is faithful and true!

Expect The Unexpected!

And I've saved the best for next to last... Finally, Christian, expect the unexpected! God's favor is going to shift your life in new and unexpected ways! Let me warn you now: walking in favor will mean unexpected opportunities! It will also mean non-negotiable requirements! Stepping into the favor of God will immediately put you in position to receive unexpected blessing, as well. God s notorious for showing up and showing out, sometimes when we least expect it!

I learned that God truly does monitor the desires of our heart. Any given time, He may decide to give you something you secretly wish or yearn for, but never asked for. Perhaps you didn't want to appear selfish before the Lord, or perhaps you thought the desire was silly or irrelevant. My friends, you're about to learn that your God loves you enough to give you things He knows you want, without you ever having to ask! He is the God who grants the desires of our hearts. What an incredible manifestation of His favor! - *Psalm 37:4*

Expect The Lord To Use You (Listen for His voice...)

The Lord may ask you to do very specific things in order to demonstrate your faith. He may ask you to do certain things in order to prepare yourself for a coming blessing He desires to release to you. Be obedient! Whenever the Lord asks you to 'trim the fat' or 'walk out your faith' so to speak, it's because He's about to do something in your life!

The Scripture that comes to mind is *Isaiah 43:19*, which says: *Behold, I will do a new thing. Now it shall spring forth; shall you not know it? I will even make a road in the wilderness and rivers in the desert.*
God constantly wants to do new things in our lives; walking in favor will mean new doors opening unto you!

The Lord may also ask you to pray for someone, bless someone unexpectedly, or prophesy over someone. I urge you to be obedient and fulfill all such requests. Remember, the Lord's favor will bless you so that you can bless others!

Several examples come to mind, such as the time Holy Spirit told me to bless someone financially. At the time, I was not overflowing in financial abundance, but I had faith in my

God. I obediently put the instructed amount of cash into an envelope and gave it to the person I was told to bless. The woman began to cry, stating that her household was in dire straits, unable to pay their bills or acquire groceries for a Thanksgiving dinner. My heart was immediately warmed as we hugged and rejoiced together at the Lord's goodness. However, I would be remiss if I did not mention that within days, that money supernaturally came back to me.

Imagine if I had not obeyed. Neither the family, nor I, would have been blessed.

Friend, your obedience is vital to your walk with the Lord!

There have been times the Lord has told me to prophesy to strangers in public. There times, God has told me to go somewhere. Each and every time, there was a reason, and I was blessed for my obedience.

Remember always, extreme obedience often releases extreme blessings! I pray many beautiful and extreme blessings of the Lord overtake and color your life!

My friend, expect the unexpected! Walking in favor means walking hand in hand with the supernatural. With the Holy Ghost involved, anything can happen! God will desire to use you, He may desire to send you, and He will bless you for it for He is a most generous and benevolent God!

This Is Going To Change Your Life Forever

Perhaps like me, you've had a rocky past. Perhaps like me, you had a difficult childhood. But even if you didn't, the Lord's favor is going to change your life, beautifully, exponentially.

I will never forget growing up as the only child in a single parent household. My mother worked hard and did what she could to raise me well, but finances were extremely limited. We were often at a disadvantage, dependent upon the generosity of others. On top of that, my mother wrestled with mental illness and generational curses.

These are the very things that cripple some people, let's be honest. There are some who succumb to the darkness of poverty, and never come out. There are some who descend into the pit of a generational curse, and never claw their way out of that pit.

But not me, and not you.
We are overcomers.
We are of a royal bloodline.
We're King's kids!

God has given us new life and freedom through Christ Jesus, and now He's calling *you* to more. Now, the Lord is calling you to step into His favor!

Stepping into God's favor is going to change you, forever. You're going to see that you have a loving and faithful Heavenly Father who really does love you. You're going to see for yourself just how much God believes in you, and desires to bless you.

You're going to see that where you come from, is not where you're going. And yes, you're going to see that your history does not have to determine your destiny!

You, Christian, are going to see that everything in your past truly has prepared you for your future, and that future is dazzling and brilliant because as a child of God, you have access to God's favor!

Stepping into favor changed me, forever. I can't erase my childhood memories, but I know I'm never going back.

I can't erase past struggles and my encounters with discrimination, abuse, rejection and poverty, but I now live in another land.

Now I live as a member of a royal priesthood, serving Christ Jesus, on my way to the Kingdom of God! *And so do you.*

Now I live knowing that my God shall supply all my needs according to His riches in glory by Christ Jesus! - *Philippians 4:19*

God is going to do the same for you. He's going to renew you, redirect you, refresh you, and bless you with His favor. And yes, Christian, it's going to change your life forever.

God bless you!

- JoLynne Whittaker

About The Author

JoLynne Whittaker is devoted to serving the Lord via her full-time ministry alongside her husband Jon. Mrs. Whittaker is known for her accurate prophetic words, dreams and visions, which she has been receiving from the Lord since she was a child.

Her former career in publishing, radio and television provide a skill set from which she draws when crafting her sermons and writing. With an intense desire to help people, JoLynne is passionate about bringing a living and powerful Jesus to a dying and disempowered world.

Visit the author online at:

JoLynneWhittaker.org

SteppingIntoFavor.com